GEORGE LEIGH MALLORY

Underwood & Underwood photographers New York.   Emery Walker ph.sc.

George Leigh-Mallory. 1923

GEORGE LEIGH MALLORY

A MEMOIR BY
DAVID PYE

WITH A FOREWORD BY
GEORGE MALLORY II

INTRODUCTION BY
TRISTRAM PYE

Orchid Press
Bangkok 2002

David Randall Pye
GEORGE LEIGH MALLORY

First published: 1927
by the Oxford University Press
London: Humphrey Milford
©David Randall Pye 1960
©Tristram Robert Pye 2002

Republished: 2002
by Orchid Press
P.O. Box 19,
Yuttitham Post Office,
Bangkok, 10907 Thailand

This book is printed on acid-free long life paper which meets the specifications of ISO 9706/1994

ISBN 974-524-010-9

Foreword

On the 13th May 1995, Alison Hargreaves reached the summit of Mount Everest without using bottled oxygen or Sherpa support: a mighty achievement by any standard. On her way back down the north ridge she stopped outside my tent, for a cup of tea and a chat. It was the afternoon before my own attempt on Everest, and Alison's success was for me inspiring and very encouraging.

Some months earlier I had memorized the final paragraph of David Pye's memoir of my grandfather (from which the text on the back cover of this book is taken) and I tried to recite it to Alison. But the lack of oxygen at 8,300 metres muddled my thoughts, and my attempt deteriorated into a shambles. When my friends and I climbed Everest the next day, our ascent went without incident. We used the same route as Alison, and the one that Mallory and Irvine had pioneered 71 years before. We had perfect weather, better equipment, bottled oxygen and we climbed the Chinese ladder at the second step, so there was nothing remarkable about what we did. We knew a great deal about the challenge we were up against, whereas Mallory and Irvine were 'moving up slowly, intelligently, into regions of unknown striving', unaware of the technical difficulties ahead of them.

A copy of this memoir had been given to me some months before my trip to Everest, and by then I was familiar with my grandfather's story. Although I had read his biography by my uncle David Robertson, and most of the many other books about him and Everest, what fascinated me here was that David Pye and Mary Anne O'Malley really knew him personally. The circumstances in which he joined the 1924 Everest expedition have been well covered, but it is a subject that continually intrigues me, and Pye really lays bare the forces which were tugging him in opposite directions: his desire to stay at home with his young family, against pressure from the Everest Committee and the lure of the highest summit in the world. The notes by Geoffrey Winthrop Young in the introduction to this memoir confirm how Mallory, so resolute when in action, in fact allowed this critical decision to be made for him.

What would David Pye have thought of the manner in which the discovery of Mallory's body in 1999 was handled? As a close friend of Mallory, and with his love of the mountains, he might well have echoed my own feelings: I was simply appalled at the immediate sale of photos of my grandfather's broken body to the international media and the way his personal possessions were treated as artifacts that might help rewrite history. The public condemnation of the climbers' behavior by Sir Edmund Hillary, Sir Chris Bonington, and many other respected mountaineers, was however of great comfort to me. The uproar has lead to the Alpine Club drafting guidelines to assist climbers dealing with similar situations in future.

Whilst it is true that in the broader public mind Everest is the only mountain that counts, I do not believe Mallory's status can be ascribed solely to his association with the mountain and the incessant quest to know whether he and Irvine reached the summit. His friends, family, and many mountaineers at the time, did not really mind how high on the mountain they had climbed; and in 1999 David Breashears declared in *Last Climb* that perhaps 'all this emphasis on the summit is to miss the point entirely'. Readers of this memoir will find that there was much more to Mallory than a mountaineer who provided a 'symbol of the invincibility of the human spirit'.

May 2002 *George Mallory II*
Melbourne, Australia *(George Christopher Leigh Mallory)*

INTRODUCTION TO THIS 2002 EDITION

George Leigh Mallory and Andrew Irvine died on Everest in 1924. Mallory's body was found on the mountain in 1999, but it may never be known if they reached the summit.

Three massive tomes totalling 16 cm in thickness, to which Mallory himself contributed 250 pages, describe fully the British Mount Everest Expeditions of 1921, 1922 and 1924. A concise account of all three expeditions was also compiled by Sir Francis Younghusband in 1926.

The expeditions were thus well documented, but a more personal memoir of Mallory was wanted by his family, friends and fellow climbers, and also by the general public: in those days of Empire, and with a war just won, he was widely regarded as a national hero who had given his life to extend the horizons of mankind. As a London paper wrote at the time, 'The spirit which animated the attacks on Everest is the same as that which has prompted Arctic and other expeditions, and in earlier times led to the formation of the Empire itself'. There was no shortage of material for a memoir, but an author was needed who could best blend reminiscences of Mallory's childhood, schooldays and mountaineering prowess, into a tribute which would fittingly reflect a man loved and admired by so many.

Who might have written this memoir?

Geoffrey Winthrop Young was ten years senior to George Mallory, and as the leading mountaineer of his day and organizer of the famous Pen y Pass parties in Wales did more than anyone to develop his climbing skills. At Cambridge he complemented Arthur Benson as Mallory's academic guide and mentor. The climbing community would probably have preferred Young to have written this memoir, but he declined to do so, as noted in the back of his copy:

'I suppose I should have written this book; and Ruth [Mallory] pressed me to. I did not, because I felt I had known George too well to get him in proper perspective, and in a relationship which did not allow of my easily changing into appreciator and appraiser. For he had been, both in the hills and in education, my 'pupil', and the initiative had always lain with me.

'After the war, he developed immensely, both as man and as mountaineer; and in this phase I could no longer observe or take part. Thus I should, in writing, have been too biased by my pre-war intimacy. I hoped that David Pye would be able to give a juster appreciation, because in better perspective: since both as contemporary and as lesser mountaineer, he would see George on the right inclination, for admiring summing up.'

Another potential author for a memoir of Mallory was **Mary Anne O'Malley**. As 'Cottie' Sanders before her marriage, she had been an early climbing companion of Mallory at the Pen y Pass climbing gatherings. She was arrestingly attractive, and many friends expected them to marry; but she succumbed instead to rising diplomat (Sir) Owen O'Malley, and married him in 1916. Mary Anne O'Malley remained a close friend of Mallory, and later achieved considerable fame as a novelist, writing under the pen name of Ann Bridge – *Peking Picnic* was a best-seller in the early 1930s. She had written her own beautifully crafted and very personal memoir of Mallory. Although never intended to be published, it might have formed the basis of a biography; but there were many who doubted whether a woman could write convincingly about the largely male preserve of mountaineering. Thus Arthur Benson, Mallory's tutor at Cambridge, said that he 'never thought a woman could write a biography'. Another objected to the opening of the O'Malley manuscript as reading 'like a novelette', and her description of life at The Holt as 'much too unrestrained'. Fortunately, such criticisms were ignored, and these passages are included untouched in the memoir: they in particular provide an immediate and vivid image of the young George Mallory, and of the happy household which he and his wife created at Charterhouse.

Between the 1922 and 1924 expeditions to Everest, George Mallory had taken a new job in Cambridge, back among many of his student and climbing companions. When he died, Ruth was supported in her grief by Mary Anne O'Malley, and also by **David Pye**, one of her late husband's closest friends.

Pye had been a contemporary of Mallory at Cambridge, but was different from him in so many ways that perhaps they found a complement in each other. Pye was an engineer and academic; Mallory read history, and was less successful academically. They shared a love of mountains, where Mallory's boundless energy and impulsiveness were countered by Pye, always deliberate and careful in thought and movement.

Mary Anne O'Malley's personal diary will now relate how in fact it was she and David Pye who came to write this memoir together.

'In July of last year [1924] I went with Ruth to pack up Herschel House. George had been dead some seven weeks, and of course my head and heart were full only of her, and how best to keep as close to her as I possibly could. Each morning we went to the house and stayed all day, going through clothes and toys and packing glass and china, and sorting linen and letters and papers. On the afternoon of the first day we were sitting on the floor in the study, Ruth going through papers and I packing them up, when David Pye came walking in. When Ruth had told me he would be coming I was just conscious of being bored at the prospect. But I knew what he was being to Ruth, so nothing else mattered.

'I saw a certain amount of David in those three days, and was taken into their counsels as to who should write George's life. And then he and I sat down with a list of people who were to be given books as keepsakes. That gave us, in the shortest shorthand the formula, so to speak, of each other's judgment of books and people. And throughout all preliminaries were cut, absolutely. We both knew Ruth very well; we were there only to help her. We stood one on each side of her, in the same relationship as her friends, who did not count at all, except for her.

'During the autumn I saw of course a lot of Ruth. She often talked of David, and I asked him to stay. We drove to Puttenham Common and sat in the heather in the sun, and began at once to talk about Ruth and the Life [of Mallory]. He found it a very hard job to tackle; there was so little to say, he said. I countered this with vigour and explained why I thought it 'psychologically exciting'. At last he burst out "Why on earth don't you do it yourself?" We got home to find Ruth, and spent a desultory evening in talk. By the time he left I had promised to look up my old diaries and write down what I could for him, as material to work on in the memoir.

'The next thing was that Ruth and I made a pilgrimage to

Cambridge to talk it all over with David. Oh, what a lovely place Trinity is! Ruth was abstracted. She and I, and no doubt he, had the same thing on our minds, wearing its individual aspect to each. David, I know, felt that I could do something goodish with the memoir; and equally that he could do much better himself, if he used such stuff as I could put up, than he could alone. Ruth wanted it done, and I was the only person who had shown any real keenness for the job – on the other hand she wanted George's friends satisfied, and felt that they would be better pleased with a David memoir.

'We went to a concert together, and came back through the little passage out of Jesus Lane, where the lamplight shows the figure whose attitude has a look of George about it, and through the Great Gate and into David's white room, and the firelight, and tea. I think David began. He praised what I had written, and I like to recall that, because then already I felt his judgment valuable, and that his praise would never be given insincerely. He objected greatly to using what I had written, because he would want at once to pull it about, and yet use some of it as it stood. I explained the only important thing was to have a good Life, and for Ruth to be satisfied. Later I met her alone and had a chance to tell her that I hoped it would be all right, and that David would do it.

'Ruth came to call on me, and said David had definitely taken on the job. She was relieved, happy, moved, saying "I know you would have liked to do it, Mary Anne, and I should have liked you to. But this is a better way. You can help David a lot, and make a better thing of it than he could alone. I know it isn't the honour or glory you want". We kissed, and went out to our walk, happy and free at heart.'

Over the next few months, Mary Anne O'Malley and David Pye worked on the memoir together, and a comparison of their manuscripts shows that about a fifth of hers was incorporated untouched. From her diary, it is evident that she fell very much in love with him. Unhappily married with three small children, she wrote 'Of course I am always hopelessly at the mercy of affection or admiration. I was pleased that David should like me, that anyone should. I would at any time take affection from any hand as a starving man would take bread'. Once when discussing the memoir, David asked 'How much were you in love with George?', to which she replied 'I was prepared to be to any extent – in fact I suppose I was; I always thought it so clever and kind of him not to make me altogether, you know'. David Pye probably did return her affection but, in those more prudish times, both must have seen that an 'affair' – between a university lecturer and the wife of a prominent diplomat – would have been a disaster for all concerned.

Later that year Owen O'Malley was appointed counsellor in a diplomatic mission to China, and the family left for Peking. David Pye and Mary Anne O'Malley corresponded frequently about the memoir until publication by the Oxford University Press and Humphrey Milford. It was reviewed on 21 June 1927 by *The Times,* who also reprinted their review in 1999 after Mallory's body had been found, under the heading 'On This Day':

GEORGE LEIGH MALLORY

A Memoir by David Pye (Milford, 10s. 6d. net).

IT IS common knowledge that George Mallory, together with Andrew Irvine, died on Everest in 1924, though how they died has not been ascertained. The gallantry of the attempt and the mystery in which it ended have associated the name of Mallory, the leader, with climbing in the minds of thousands who knew nothing of him or mountaineering. But to those who have read the three books which were written about the expeditions to Everest, Mallory is something more than a climber. He stood for the whole party in an undertaking in which the ascent of Everest stood for the Ascent of Man. His failures lent themselves to the conception not less than his successes. From his poignantly lucid account of the conditions in which the seven porters lost their lives one can realize how insidious was the trap set by Everest for a man of his temperament.

There must have been a widespread desire among those who knew of him only as a climber to learn more of him as a man; and this has been met by Mr. Pye, in whose admirably written account Mallory is the more alive as an individual and the more typical of his class and generation for no attempt being made to conceal his shortcomings. It makes it probable that if he exhibited in Tibet the affectations of his younger days, he would have been a critical and unsatisfactory subordinate: and also that the metal of which his intimate friends knew him to be composed would shine bright and ring true when action had scoured off the rust on the surface. His vision was concentrated on what was big and beautiful and distant and vague; it took a mountain to make him watch his feet on the moraine immediately in front of him.

The memoir has been extensively quoted in most books about Everest and Mallory: it is mentioned more than 100 times in those which have appeared since the 1999 expedition, but most readers have - until now - been unable to consult references, as the 1927 edition was never reprinted, and second-hand copies are costly and hard to find.

Comments by Geoffrey Winthrop Young

It has already been mentioned that Young was originally asked to write this memoir, and will have made several contributions to it. In his copy he wrote several notes which are of interest.

The first few pages describing Mallory in Zermatt were in fact written by Mary Anne O'Malley, and Mallory's 'companion' [page 1] was Young himself, who made the introduction to 'Cottie' Sanders, as she then was.

There is an apocryphal story that Mallory's Slab Climb in Wales was first discovered by him climbing solo to retrieve a pipe [p.4]. This made a good anecdote, but Young maintained that they had together surveyed this route on the previous day.

Mallory indeed had a gift for leadership [p.50], but Young remarked: 'Yes, but not until Everest days. His earlier idea of leadership was to go over the top at the first rush. He lacked the detachment of an officer'.

When climbing Mallory could be impetuously decisive, but this contrasts curiously with his vacillation when it came to participating in the Everest expeditions. Young noted [p.106] that before 1921 'what happened was that George left it to Ruth. She was against it. He was going to refuse. I saw them both together, and in 20 minutes' talk Ruth saw what I meant: how much the 'label' of Everest would mean to his career, and educational plans. She told him to go. Pye has it here all wrong.'[!]. And when invited on the 1924 expedition [p.144] Young said it was his personal opinion that Mallory would have been profoundly relieved if the expedition had been called off [p.145], and that he had advised him <u>not</u> to go. Mallory was not 'happy' about this: Young noted that 'what he meant was that he was happy that the decision had been taken out of his hands'.

When it came to choosing who should join the 1922 Expedition [p.107], 'Mallory himself picked out his old schoolfellow Bullock to go, practically without asking agreement'. The memoir relates [p.130] how in that year Mallory was leading four porters on a rope across a slope, when all slipped past him. Young commented: 'It was a remarkable save, especially in descent. He held all four!'

On the cover of his copy of the memoir, Young noted that 'George only became wholly his radiant self when in strong action, with mind and body in swift motion. The romantic myth of Mallory as he was in action is likely to be the memory of him that survives'.

Young took up mountaineering again after losing a leg in the 1914-18 war: his more remarkable feats included climbing the Matterhorn and the Aiguille du Grépon with an artificial leg. As noted in the Pen y Pass Book (four albums of photographs, sketches and anecdotes recording the climbing parties from 1907-1947), 'Young was labouring slowly up Great Gable on 8 June 1924 to dedicate a memorial to those climbers fallen in the first war. He spoke from the summit rock, after a bugle call; and the words were audible upon Green Gable, through the rain and clouds, parting into sunshine. [This ceremony] was, very actually, Mallory's Requiem' – because, unbeknown to Young and the party of more than 500 others who were present, it was the very day on which Mallory and Irvine were last seen on Everest.

Who contributed to this memoir?

Notes in his copy of the memoir show that Young was disappointed that his name had not been mentioned more often. But there were so many others who had helped – such as Mallory's family, staff and students at Winchester, Cambridge and Charterhouse, and fellow climbers – that Pye decided to make almost no acknowledgements; if he had done so, he would probably have offended many more who were not mentioned, and by eschewing quotations and footnotes he was able to write a seamless and homogeneous narrative. The brief acknowledgement given in the memoir to the contribution made by Mary Anne O'Malley was, in the opinion of her daughter Jane, no less than she would have wished. There are several cases where letters from Mallory to others appear to have been written to the author, but Pye was by nature modest and unassuming, and would not have wanted to embellish the part he had played in the life of his friend.

Did Mallory and Irvine reach the summit?

In his 1986 book *The Mystery of Mallory and Irvine*, Tom Holzel asked why Pye and Robertson had not addressed this question more directly: 'A great explorer dies a famous death, and neither of his biographers wants to talk about it'. But Robertson began by declaring that his was not an 'expedition book'; he had available every possible resource for his scholarly biography, and wisely refrained from empty conjecture. And Pye was writing in the aftermath of months of investigation by the Mount Everest Committee as to what had actually happened, interviews with eye-witnesses, and speculation by the press - what we would now call 'media mania'. His was an affectionate memoir, dedicated to Mallory's widow and children, and there was little he could add to all the official reports of the expedition: but he certainly believed that Mallory, obsessed by Everest, would have been unable to resist risking a last bid for the 'sun-bathed summit beckoning to them 800 feet above (and that looks little enough); can we see them turning back?'

'Because it is there'

When Everest was climbed by Sir Edmund Hillary and Sherpa

Tenzing in 1953, interest was revived in earlier attempts on the mountain, and Mallory's often-quoted reply to the question 'Why climb Everest?' came up again. My father told me that, after his trip to America in 1923, Mallory denied that he had ever said 'Because it is there' - or that if he had, he had been impatiently reacting to an exasperating reporter: he never suffered fools gladly. But whether from him or not, his alleged reply has since acquired the status of a mystic and philosophical epigram, and it does express rather well Mallory's attitude to the challenge of high mountains.

Acknowledgements

I have received considerable help and encouragement in getting this new edition to print. My particular thanks go to Joanna Gordon for permission to quote from the manuscript biography of George Mallory and diary by Mary Anne O'Malley, of whom she is legatee. A copy of the manuscript was provided by the University of Texas (see bibliography) and compared with this memoir, but was not quoted directly. I am indebted to Jocelin Winthrop Young for lending me his father's annotated copy of the memoir and the Pen y Pass Book, and to Peter and Leni Gillman, authors of *The Wildest Dream*, in particular for help with the bibliography which follows. The Times gave me permission to print their 1927 review of the book, and I am also indebted to the Alpine Club and Royal Geographical Society, for whom in 1925 the Ordnance Survey reproduced the fine map of Mount Everest shown on the front cover.

April 2002,   *Tristram Pye*
Freising, Germany

SELECTED BIBLIOGRAPHY:
MALLORY AND EVEREST

1922 Charles Howard-Bury, George Mallory et al: *Everest Reconnaissance 1921*, Edward Arnold

1924 C.G.Bruce, George Mallory et al: *The Assault on Everest 1922*, Edward Arnold

1925 Edward Norton et al: *The Fight for Everest 1924*, Edward Arnold

1925 Mary Anne O'Malley: *Biography of George Leigh Mallory*, 106 page manuscript in Harry Ransom Humanities Research Center of the University of Texas at Austin

1926 Sir Francis Younghusband: *The Epic of Mount Everest*, Edward Arnold. (Republished by Trafalgar Square, 2001. German translation entitled *Bis zur Spitze des Mount Everest* republished by Sport Verlag Berlin, 2000)

1927 David Pye: *George Leigh Mallory*, Oxford University Press and Humphrey Milford (First edition of this book)

1957 Geoffrey Winthrop Young et al: *Snowdon Biography*, J.M.Dent

1969 David Robertson: *George Mallory*, Faber and Faber, republished by Orchid Press, 1999. (This was the first full biography, by Mallory's son-in-law)

1986 David Robertson: *Mallory's Climbs before Everest*, Monograph

1986 Tom Holzel and Audrey Salkeld: *The Mystery of Mallory and Irvine*, Jonathan Cape (Republished by Pimlico, 1999)

1990 Dudley Green: *Mallory of Everest*, Faust Publishing Company

1991 Walt Unsworth: *Everest*, Grafton

1993 Peter Gillman (Editor): *Everest: The Best Writings and*

Pictures, Little, Brown

1993 Audrey Salkeld and John Boyle: *Climbing Mount Everest: The Bibliography*, Sixways

1996 Alan Hankinson: *Geoffrey Winthrop Young: Poet, Mountaineer, Educator*, Hodder & Stoughton

1999 Conrad Anker and David Roberts: *The Lost Explorer*, Simon and Schuster

1999 Jochen Hemmleb et al: *Ghosts of Everest*, The Mountaineers Books

1999 Peter Firstbrook: *Lost on Everest: The Search for Mallory & Irvine*, National Geographic

1999 David Breashears and Audrey Salkeld: *Last Climb*, National Geographic (Includes a foreword by John Mallory, son of George Leigh Mallory, and a contribution by George Mallory II)

1999 David Roberts: *Out of Thin Air*, National Geographic Adventure (Fall 1999)

1999 Conrad Anker: *Mystery on Everest*, National Geographic (October 1999)

1999 Reinhold Messner: *Mallory's Zweiter Tod*, BLV (Translation *'The Second Death of George Mallory'* published by St. Martin's Press, 2001)

2000 Peter and Leni Gillman: *The Wildest Dream*, Headline Book Publishing   (Biography of George Mallory)

2000 Audrey Salkeld and Conrad Anker: *Mystery on Everest: Photobiography of George Mallory*, National Geographic

2000 Peter and Leni Gillman (editors): *Everest: Eighty Years of Triumph and Tragedy*, Little, Brown (Updated edition of 1993 anthology)

2000 Julie Summers: *Fearless on Everest*, Weidenfeld and Nicholson (Biography of Andrew Irvine, with additional material about George Mallory)

THE AUTHOR OF THIS MÉMOIR

DAVID RANDALL PYE
(1886-1960)

Mallory and Pye were born in the same year; they first met as students at Cambridge University, and often went climbing together. After graduating in record time with first-class honours in Mechanical Sciences, Pye helped start the faculty of engineering science at Oxford. He was an experimental officer and pilot in the Royal Flying Corps during the First World War, and spent some time as assistant master at Winchester College, where Mallory had been a scholar ten years previously. Both Pye and Mallory had progressive ideas about education, and together with Geoffrey Winthrop Young considered starting a school, an idea which might have come to fruition but for the Everest disaster.

After the war, Pye returned to Cambridge as a lecturer, and did important research on internal combustion engines. He was Director of Scientific Research at the Air Ministry during WW2, later resuming an academic career as Provost of University College in London. He was appointed CB and FRS in 1937 and knighted in 1952, and in the same year became President of the Institution of Mechanical Engineers.

Pye was an enthusiastic and competent mountaineer and skier in the Alps, and made several first ascents in Britain. A party including Mallory and his young wife explored Skye in 1919, but it was left to Pye to lead the first ascent of the severe Crack of Doom after climbing the Cioch Direct. Those who have served an apprenticeship on the Idwal Slabs in Wales will know Faith, Hope and Charity: after Hope was climbed in 1915, Pye completed this trinity the following year with first ascents of Faith and Charity. He was elected to the Alpine Club in 1922, proposed by George Mallory and seconded by Geoffrey Winthrop Young, and elected Vice-President in 1956.

Between the world wars, Pye scarcely missed a climbing or skiing season in the Alps, and whilst at University College did much to encourage the new generation of post-war climbers.

To
RUTH MALLORY
for
CLARE
BERIDGE
and
JOHN

PREFACE

IN putting together this memoir of my friend George Mallory the help I have received has been too widespread to make individual acknowledgement possible. But there must be two exceptions: the late Mr. Arthur Benson and Mrs. Owen O'Malley. My debt to the former for details of Cambridge days will be evident in Chapter II. Without the co-operation of Mrs. O'Malley the book in its present form would scarcely have been possible at all.

I am indebted to the Mount Everest Committee for permission to make use of the two photographs which face pages 114 and 129.

CONTENTS

I. Introductory *page* 1
II. Cambridge Days 9
III. The Mountaineer 26
IV. Charterhouse 55
V. The War 81
VI. Everest:
The Reconnaissance and Assault 99
VII. Everest:
The Last Adventure 136

LIST OF ILLUSTRATIONS

George Mallory 1923	*Frontispiece*
George Mallory at the age of twenty	*to face page* 9
On the Moine ridge of the Aiguille Verte, 1909	44
G. M. with his elder daughter, Clare, 1917	77
The North-western aspect of Everest from the Rongbuk glacier	114
Mallory and Norton at near 27,000 feet	129

I
INTRODUCTORY

UNDISTURBED by the chatter and movement of the crowd on the terrace of the Monte Rosa hotel at Zermatt, a young man was sitting immersed in a book. He seemed oblivious of the ebb and flow of the human tide, until presently a companion appeared from the hotel and roused him for an introduction. He got up at once and went through it adequately, although with a certain restiveness. The moment courtesy permitted he relapsed into his iron chair and his book, never looking up, only sometimes raising a hand to push back the shock of brown hair which fell constantly over his forehead. The young man was George Mallory, the time August 1909, his third season in the Alps. He was picturesque and untidy, in loose grey flannels with a bright handkerchief round his neck. A typical undergraduate, rather conscious, probably, of his appearance and yet with a detachment about himself which placed him at once outside the class of those who are self-conscious in any derogatory sense. It would never have occurred to him to think of himself as more good-looking than other people, but he would have regarded it as mere humbug to pretend that good looks were not a source of satisfaction just as real as the possession of splendid limbs and a strong wind: all blessings to be thankfully

GEORGE LEIGH-MALLORY

accepted but calling for no comment. Perhaps his restiveness in the presence of strangers might be traced to a subconscious fear of this comment, even though unspoken, for its occurrence was inevitable. His features were singularly beautiful and his complexion at that date, when he was twenty-three, still as clear and fair as that of a boy of thirteen. This in itself would have made his appearance remarkable, more especially among climbers that season, for it was a bad one with much new snow, and faces disfigured by sunburn were the rule.

His companion that year was Geoffrey Winthrop Young, a name already known throughout the Alps among climbers for his daring and successful new ascents, so that Mallory must have felt himself even then well on the way to acceptance among the front rank of climbers. Rumour as to what they had done and were going to attempt had preceded them at Zermatt and now comment flowed about them. The old guard were critical, a little amused, on the whole a little hostile, though some were prepared to be generous to what was still a new school of mountaineering. It was surprising what an amount of information or invention was circulating that August about them: from the times in which they had gone up various peaks to the precise place where the more bizarre parts of their apparel had been bought. Mallory was not much in evidence. A good deal of his time was spent in his iron chair with a book. He was not really unsociable, and not in the least difficult to make friends with, nor to talk to as soon as the conversation showed signs of ranging beyond

INTRODUCTORY

the common circle of topography and personalities. The subject of mountains—the quality of their beauty and the climbers's reaction to it—so roused him at once as to make one feel that here was the authentic thing; here at last, among so much conventional chatter, was the real flame and passion. He was intolerant of the potterers and gossip-mongers though at the same time quite modest about his own performances. He didn't mind, in fact rather enjoyed confessing, with a half shamefaced and half whimsical amusement, to his more desperate escapades. In those days his extreme youthfulness would have made it difficult to recognize in him the responsible leader he afterwards became, or to appreciate the reserve of strength which, even then, made it necessary to readjust one's standards in deciding whether, for him, a climb could be justified as sound mountaineering. One of these escapades had occurred the previous August in North Wales and has become a part of climbing history: His party had left the rocks and were homeward bound from Lliwedd when it was discovered that Mallory had left his pipe on a ledge half-way up the face, where the party had lunched. There are to be found comparatively easy ways of reaching the ledge from below such as the normal man would employ late in the day, and for the recovery of a pipe. Not so George Mallory. When he rejoined the others at the hotel it was discovered that he had not merely omitted to take the easy route but had invented an entirely new way of reaching the ledge, up a particularly steep and exposed slab, his excuse being that it was the most

GEORGE LEIGH-MALLORY

direct way up! The 'Slab-Climb' remains one of the most sensational on the Lliwedd face and, contrary to custom, is distinguished by the name of its discoverer.

That Mallory should so early have made a mark in the climbing world was due largely to his good fortune in going to Winchester. Few men have the chance of serious climbing before they leave school, but at Winchester Mallory met Mr. R. L. G. Irving and was introduced by him at the age of eighteen to guideless climbing in the Alps. He was already a fine gymnast, and from the first his perfect balance and adventurous agility carried him on from one triumph to another. Indeed it was revealed later on to Mr. Irving, who was at that time tutor in College at Winchester, that during the summer term before their first expedition to the Alps, Mallory had gone with a companion to practise on the ruins of Wolvesey Palace opposite the College, and that on the unexpected collapse of a piece of the wall it was only by a leap of several yards that an accident had been avoided.

But there were times before this adventurousness had its complement of self-reliance, born of skill and experience, and in earlier days the young George must have given anxious moments to those who looked after him. His father, the Rev. Herbert Leigh-Mallory, was both clergyman and Lord of the Manor at the village of Mobberley in Cheshire at the time of George's birth on the 18th of June 1886. He was the eldest of four children, two boys and two girls, and it is of interest to record that the spirit of adventure which took the elder brother to the

INTRODUCTORY

mountains carried the younger through a brilliant flying career in which he was one of the pioneers, during the war, in the development of low altitude 'contact' flying in co-operation with infantry. At Mobberley all their childhood was spent, for it was not until 1904, when George was eighteen, that his family moved to Birkenhead on his father's becoming vicar of St. John's parish there. I have said that he was fortunate in going to Winchester and in being taken by Mr. Irving to the Alps, but one can scarcely doubt that the development in him of the mountaineer would have been in any case only a matter of time. Unconscious memory of an arboreal past is apt to show itself early, and in most of us who have once felt the joy of controlled poise and secure balance in unsafe places the climbing instinct is a driving force not to be denied. It is recorded that already at the age of seven George Mallory, banished from the nursery at tea-time for unruly behaviour and sent to his own room, was at last discovered climbing about on the church roof. ' I did go to my room,' he protested, ' to fetch my cap.'

Walls, roofs, and trees seemed to be his natural playground. No very unusual one, it is true, but it is of a certain interest to find that at this early age he was scarcely affected by any sense of personal danger. A year or so after the escapade on the church roof his family were at St. Bees for the summer holidays. One exceptionally rough day George announced his intention to stay upon a certain rock while the sea came in and surrounded it, and to remain marooned there until the tide went down. Before any one responsible was aware of what he was up to, the water was swirling and tumbling among the rocks around him, it was quite impossible for him to get back, and it was clear that waves would soon be breaking over the highest part of the rock which he was on. His grandmother gave the alarm and a young man volunteered to rescue him. The situation must have been serious, for the man made repeated unsuccessful attempts before reaching the rock. When he did so however he was astonished to find this boy of eight or nine perfectly calm and unafraid. On another occasion about the same time his mother was only in time to discover him when he had already climbed nearly to the top of a high iron pier, and had to wait at the bottom while he returned, quite deliberately and with perfect composure. There is no doubt that all his life he enjoyed taking risks, or perhaps it would be fairer to say doing things with a small margin of safety. He always caught a train by five seconds rather than five minutes: a trait annoying to his companions, and not less so because he always justified it by not missing the train. A dislike of waste, whether of space or time, kept him constantly on the look-out for ' short cuts '. And it was the same trait, probably, which made him a dashing rather than a good driver of motor-cars. He confessed that he never could resist the temptation to try to overtake any car which he could see in front; and having caught it up he would probably pass it with a minimum of clearance, just as he rounded every corner in such a way as not to waste energy, as he said, in regaining

INTRODUCTORY

lost speed. In fairness to him I must add that he never had to my knowledge any serious accident.

At the age of eleven he was sent to Glengorse Preparatory School, Eastbourne. Here, after a year or two, he distinguished himself by running away. Not because he was homesick or otherwise unhappy, but to oblige a friend! The other truant, it seems, felt a need for moral support in the enterprise and George agreed to keep him company. The two got as far as a Church Lads Brigade shelter where they were hospitably, if guilefully, entertained while the school was communicated with. On the arrival of an assistant master to take them back it was found that George in the act of flight had been unable to face parting with his geometry books and that his luggage consisted simply of these, done up in brown paper with a strap! He agreed to return on the condition that he was not beaten when they got back: a promise which was easily given and then, to George's infinite disgust, at once broken on their arrival.

In 1900 he won a scholarship at Winchester and entered College there in September of that year. Although he did not distinguish himself particularly either at games or athletics, he played for College Six and used to speak of the enjoyment and the self-reliance he had derived from football at Winchester. Evidently while at school it occupied his mind a good deal, and again, during the war, the standard he had then set himself was invoked as a measure of conduct in sterner surroundings. 'In turning over and weighing my own personal courage,' he wrote

GEORGE LEIGH-MALLORY

in 1916, 'I have found myself repeating words from one of the little sad volumes of Artillery Training . . . " such a complete absence of self-interest, that he will do his duty in the hour of danger *coolly and accurately* " '—and he goes on to reflect that he is taken back, for reassurance, to football days at Winchester.

He was, as I have said, a fine gymnast, of the lithe rather than the heavily muscled type, and was also in the school shooting VIII which won the Ashburton Shield in 1904. In a letter written that same summer term we get a glimpse of the fiery energy he used later on to show among the mountains. He bicycled to Salisbury on Ascension Day to see the Cathedral and 'Eddy Morgan came with me in a trailer as he is not allowed to bike far, and as the road was up and down precipices for about 27 miles I fairly sweated'. Fifty-four miles in a day up and down hill, dragging a trailer behind; one feels that the motor-cycle has killed such Homeric feats!

He was a Woolwich candidate in 1904 but does not seem seriously to have contemplated a career in the Army. Although Mathematics had hitherto been his strongest subject he now took up History with a view to a Scholarship at Cambridge. In this he was so far successful as to obtain an Exhibition at Magdalene College in 1905, whither he went up for his first term in October of that year.

George Mallory at the age of twenty

II

CAMBRIDGE DAYS

AT Cambridge Mallory was no less fortunate than at school in the matter of the older men with whom the chances of his education made him acquainted. Mr. Arthur Benson had, not long before, accepted the post of Supervisor in History at Magdalene, and from this association there grew, from the first days of Mallory's arrival in Cambridge, a friendship both intimate and lifelong. Mr. Benson has recounted to me the birth of their acquaintance. He had gone one Sunday morning in early October, just before the term began, to King's Chapel, and had sat in the nave for Matins. His attention was arrested during the service—there were only a few people present—by the graceful movements and demeanour of a very youthful looking undergraduate in a new gown who sat just in front of him, and by the reverence he showed, standing and kneeling in due order when most of the leisurely congregation remained seated all through. He was still more struck, when the young man turned to leave the Chapel, with the extraordinary and delicate beauty of his face. Not long after Mr. Benson had returned to the Old Granary, where he was then living, a Mr. Mallory was announced as being one of his pupils in History, and there before him was the young man he had seen at King's.

GEORGE LEIGH-MALLORY

There were at that time about fifty men only in the College, and with such small numbers, ample opportunities for the acquaintance, thus begun, to develop. In the weekly essays for his Supervisor and in the discussions upon them which followed Mallory took the keenest interest, and often the talk would range away to other topics and over wider fields. Mr. Benson told me that he was by no means punctual in showing up these essays, which were often of great length. Several times he had to complain of this unpunctuality and on one occasion, just after one of these complaints, he found an enormous essay on his table, so late in the day that there would be no time even to read it before his pupil arrived. Meeting Mallory by chance in the court Mr. Benson spoke rather sharply about it, saying that this persistent lateness in showing up the essays destroyed his pleasure in reading them and his ability to discuss much which he would have found interesting, had he been given time to consider it. Mallory looked at him mutely, said he was very sorry, and went his way. When the hour for going through the essay arrived Mr. Benson tried to unravel the causes for the delay. It turned out that after a rather late beginning Mallory had got interested, and had actually sat up the whole night till 6.30 a.m. writing the essay! After this incident he was scrupulously punctual. He did not do well in either part of the Tripos, taking a third and a second class, but this Mr. Benson declared to me he considered to be largely his own fault owing to his having encouraged his pupil to devote much too much time to his essays, and to

CAMBRIDGE DAYS

reading which was guided more by his own preference than by a schedule. There is no doubt that Mallory enjoyed writing: he enjoyed the charm of words and he enjoyed using and manipulating them. His contributions to the published accounts of the first two Everest expeditions show that he could give a graphic account of an experience in crisp and picturesque English, but his taste leaned rather to the impassioned and the elaborate, and he had always a metaphysical hankering to get behind the surface of things—a trait which led him to be diffuse rather than economical with his words.

Apart from the work for the Tripos, Mallory and Mr. Benson were associated in the founding of a little essay club within the College, the Kingsley Club, at which papers were read and very informal debates took place. It is the peculiar quality, and the value, of such undergraduate groups that opinions hastily formed can be frankly, even crudely, expressed. They form a sort of training ground for the technique of civilized intercourse. George Mallory was at this time very contentious, a most persistent and even derisive arguer, he was apt to express himself disdainfully and contemptuously, and to shift his ground, but more because he had not got the issue clear in his mind than from mental agility. These were the faults of youth, born of an enthusiasm which got the better of his sense of humour. Though he plunged eagerly if not deeply into every kind of social and moral question, his ideas were still vague and crude, and he had a provoking way of generalizing on insufficient grounds and then insisting that

GEORGE LEIGH-MALLORY

any honest and clear-headed man must agree with him. But in spite of his impatience in argument it was impossible to be either bored or angry, for his irritability was never prolonged beyond the limits of debate. The wrangle finished, he was all friendly interest and consideration. I think he regarded debatable questions as providing a sort of intellectual fisticuffs in which you hit out as shrewdly as you could and did not resent your adversary doing the same. In all ordinary matters he was delightfully good-humoured and tolerant, perhaps a little disposed to forget or ignore engagements, but full of penitence if he found he had caused any inconvenience.

In conversation he was not always easy to follow; he talked so rapidly, and so many words got their wings clipped in the process, as to make him at times almost unintelligible. About his humour I was never certain. He delighted in anything absurd and amusing, but had not much humorous initiative nor any gift for epigram. Perhaps in these early days he was too much of a partisan and controversialist to achieve a dispassionate and contemplative point of view, and this led him to be copious rather than terse in his talk.

But for all that he had great social charm, partly from the extreme grace and beauty of his face and figure, partly through the frank and friendly cordiality of his manner, which he showed to all alike, and partly in the liveliness and animation of his mind and his very varied range of interests.

It must not be thought that with the delicacy and refinement of his face and bearing there was at this time, or ever, any touch of languor or effeminacy. He seemed always fresh, alert, in high training, and with no shadow of those elements which are often the penalties of great personal attractiveness. Compliments he brushed aside and sentiment found no echo in his spirit. His charm was not a romantic charm: he had, rather, something virginal and cold about him: it was granite and Alpine snows which could light the real flame of his spirit.

He did not distinguish himself particularly in athletics at Cambridge. Apart from the river, where he was a good oar and later on an energetic boat-captain, his activities of this kind were reserved for the vacations. The general impression conveyed by his figure and appearance was not obviously athletic or even muscular. He had the air of a walker more than of a successful player of games; his limbs were not closely knit, but rather seemed loosely put together. This, and his very free carriage and poise of the head gave him almost a lounging air as he walked, but combined with a quick and curiously easy and supple stride, a gliding motion with no rigidity or abruptness.

He rowed during all his first three years and was captain of the College boat club in the third. The time was a successful one for Magdalene, for during the year of his captaincy the College boat went up four places in the Lent races and five in the Mays. Indeed, during his first three years the College's one boat made a total of seventeen bumps and was not once bumped either in Lents or Mays. He had a passion for bathing, which he indulged with a complete disregard of temperature and circumstance; a Welsh lake at Easter, when the temperature was little above freezing, drew him as irresistibly as the river in full summer. There was one hot night in the Long Vacation when this propensity of his brought him very nearly to the police court. He insisted on diving in from a punt at a point some way below Magdalene Bridge, in spite of protests that the time was close upon ten o'clock. He refused to return to the boat, and finally the occupants made off up the river, declaring that they must return it and be in by ten o'clock. Mallory did not follow, thinking he would get into College via the Fellows' Garden. All doors proved to be locked, nor could he attract the attention of any one to help him in his need. He had not a shred of clothing, and the punt was now hopelessly out of reach. In desperation he swam across to the quayside and made a sprint, all dripping, over the bridge to the College gates. He rang furiously, but before the porter could open, a policeman came up and demanded his name. How he succeeded in soothing the man's outraged sensibilities and persuaded him to see the humour of the situation, will never be known, but succeed he did, and the policeman retired on condition that the affair was reported to the College tutor.

Another incident of about the same time was related to me by Mr. Benson. Mallory had had an accident to his knee and was forced to stay in bed. Here Mr. Benson went to see him after morning chapel on Sunday and was begged to play a game of picquet. He did so, and they had got well into their

CAMBRIDGE DAYS

game when there came a step upon the stair. Mallory, with a sudden adroit sweep of the hand, gathered up all the cards on the counterpane, where they were playing, and put a book on the top, just as the Master, Donaldson, came good-humouredly in. Mr. Benson got up and the Master sat down on the foot of the bed, and talked in a lively manner of College affairs, of men and things. The agony of suspense was plain to read on Mallory's face as he clung to the book. But presently the Master withdrew and he sank back with a look of intense relief. 'I was ever so afraid he would ask what the book was and would take it up,' he said; 'would he have been annoyed with *you*?' 'No,' Benson replied, 'you would at once have said you were playing a game of patience—but shall we go on with our game?' 'Oh, no,' replied Mallory, with a shiver of pleasant horror, 'I am far too frightened.'

During the years 1906 and 1907 Mallory began to see a good deal of the young Intelligentsia of the University. He joined the Fabian Society and became to some extent a revolutionary in his ideas. Politics in those days was in the air, and it was inevitable that Mallory, with his genuine interest in social questions and his love of argument, should be drawn into the whirlpool of undergraduate discussions on politics, art, and literature. The period corresponded, as it so often does, with a phase of self-consciousness. He took to dressing rather peculiarly in black flannel shirts and coloured ties; and grew his hair long. If remonstrated with on the grounds that he himself was the one person who

GEORGE LEIGH-MALLORY

could not contemplate or derive pleasure from the pictorial effect, he would maintain that it was a right and natural form of self-expression. At any rate it was largely a game, and did not divert him from his genuine interests, friendship, mountaineering, art, and literature.

Of the last two I feel scarcely qualified to speak; he had a great love of the pictorial and plastic arts in which I should say he showed a good deal of natural discrimination with little technical knowledge; in literature he read eagerly and devoured a great variety of books, but I doubt whether at that time he had developed much critical appreciation.

It was in the arts of friendship and mountaineering that I believe he showed genius. To him friendship really was an art. He possessed that first consideration, a lively curiosity about human beings and a sense of the wealth of interest that may be latent in some casual encounter. 'My journey was full of variety,' he says in a letter to Mr. Benson. 'At Leicester I fell in with a London parson who turned out to be a talkative bore of the worst possible kind. I escaped at Leeds, on the excuse of wanting to smoke, to the next compartment, and there I met an Oxford man who turned out to be a most delightful person. I was reading Marius, with which he was acquainted—he opened a conversation on the subject which led to the discussion of all sorts of things, so that when he got out at Carlisle it seemed incredible that I had met him so short a time before.'

Mallory had, of course, all sorts of special assets for the art of making friends. There was his extraordinary personal charm, for one thing, which created in the people he met a strong predisposition to be friends with him. But he never, so to speak, *used* this in any way. He cannot of course have been wholly unconscious of it—that would argue an impossible stupidity—but his attitude towards it (if you can call it anything so definite as an attitude) was one of complete indifference. It was, he made one feel, irrelevant. He presented to the newcomer a charming attack, just the happiest mixture of certainty and modesty, with a pleasant assumption of common interests. He invited him, as it were, to explore these a little together to see what came of it. And a good deal generally came of it; because if there weren't common interests he could almost create them by his own enthusiasms.

All this applies, of course, only to the initial stages of making friends. But friendship, properly understood, was of enormous importance to Mallory. All through his life this was true. Friendship was to him one of the first things; something to be fostered and requiring a definite technique, not to be left to the casual chance of circumstance. He was prepared to spend time, effort, thought, and patience on perfecting it, for he did not expect relationships either to come into being or to remain in good order without intelligent endeavour. This is not to say that friendship with him was an artificial or laboured thing—no one took a greater spontaneous delight in people—but he knew that spontaneity is also capricious, and he was not—that was all—prepared to leave one of the most important things in life at the mercy of caprice. He often expressed amazement at the lack of care with which people in general conducted their relationships, compared with their painstaking industry over, say, money-making. He himself laboured with a delighted artistry at this great and joyful business of his friends : understanding them, enjoying them, sharing his best pleasures with them, unstintingly; shouldering the obligations, often very onerous, as he interpreted them, of being some one's friend and equally and rightly ready to accept the good offices of his friends himself.

He would inevitably, no doubt, have cared deeply for people and been deeply cared for by them in any case; but I think the peculiar importance that he attached to this matter of friends was a good deal due to his years at Cambridge. Looking back one cannot avoid the conviction that the years from 1904 to 1910 saw the growth at Cambridge of a very remarkable group of young—and older—people, women as well as men, who between them contrived to make a notable contribution to the life of their generation. It is not their individual distinction in literature and science which I have in mind; it is rather a sort of joint contribution of which no tangible record can remain. One or two short lives of the many who are dead; one or two collections of letters privately printed; among these scanty materials, perhaps, it is possible to catch the reflection of an art of life not wholly new, but practised in a manner new to their time. Among them was to be found an attitude towards life and other human beings of a peculiar quality and flavour; a readiness for intercourse, an absolute directness of mind, a half-sceptical, half-ardent fearlessness in matters of the heart and spirit—these were the first things perhaps to show themselves. But there were other features recognizable as common, in a measure, to them all. Personal relationships were supremely important, and all conventional inessentials were meaningless to them. They were extraordinarily attached; there was, literally, nothing they would not do for one another. Delightedly they examined and explored every means of knowing people better and liking them more, from the simplest pleasures of food and exercise taken together to the final closeness of the common acceptance of some sorrow or some truth. But three things in particular stamped them as living in a manner different, at that time, from the common run of people, and show them, in retrospect, as true forerunners of the twentieth century. In the first place they brought their whole intellectual energy to bear on their relationships; they wanted to know, not only that they loved people, but how and why they loved them, to understand the mechanism of their likings, the springs that prompted thought and emotion; to come to terms with themselves and with one another; to know where they were going and why. At that time this passion for analysis *was* new; it looked cold-blooded; it shocked people in the poems of Rupert Brooke. And because of it, and through it, they developed a new technique—an outspokenness which was then extraordinary. There was nothing, whether simple or difficult or disquieting, that they would not express or try to express. They were right, for until a thing is expressed it cannot be understood—often not even by its creator. They ceased to be afraid of words, and this in turn carried their understanding further, since it helped to set them free from the fear of understanding what they might have been afraid to express. This outspokenness was the second distinguishing mark on them—the complete directness, the unfettered freedom, of their mind and speech. And in its turn this led on to the third, the most surprising, the most engaging, quality of all. They were unafraid of expressing their affection. This has always been a characteristic feature of a really civilized community; one of the final and most difficult achievements of human intercourse. They did it; delightedly, wittily, skilfully, seriously, with the care and zest that went to all their doings.

George Mallory was in the midst of all this; he was a feature of it, and an important contributor himself. Few of his letters of this time survive, but there are letters *to* him which show something of the part he took. And it left its mark on him, in the seriousness and conscientious care with which he dealt with his friends. It was, moreover, not only on the friendship of his contemporaries that he would expend this care and thought. The subsequent history of the acquaintance which began in King's Chapel was told to me in some detail by Mr. Benson, and it shows Mallory in so new and so individual a light as to be well worth dwelling upon.

In the year 1907 a very tragic event happened in

CAMBRIDGE DAYS

Mr. Benson's family circle, which gave him a great shock and was followed by a period of intolerable strain. All through the summer he was unable to shake off the attacks of melancholy which beset him, and at last he left Cambridge for a long rest. In October he returned, to find himself worse than ever and wholly unable to face his College work. Again he left Cambridge and did not return except in Vacations until October 1908. Even after this year of rest he was still very ill, suffering from sleeplessness and constant depression of spirits. He found he could do his work, but that was all. What he needed was quiet society; but he was not sufficiently cheerful to seek it and fancied himself a wet blanket upon all conversations and companies.

It was during this time, when Mallory was at the beginning of his fourth year, that Mr. Benson was greatly struck and touched by his behaviour. The two had not met for more than a year, and Mallory had by now a wide circle of friends of his own age. Moreover a young man, as a rule, finding himself with an older man who is suffering from morbid depression, is helpless. He does not understand what it means to be incessantly melancholy, it frightens him and deprives him of his own cheerfulness. It is not any lack of goodwill or good nature, or even of unselfishness, that makes him keep away; but if he is thrown into the company of the sufferer he is conscious of constraint on both sides, feels genuinely that he can be of no use, and ends by keeping away.

This was not the case with George Mallory. He was the only undergraduate of that time, so Mr.

Benson told me, who constantly and continually, week after week, put himself out to do what he could to help. He used to come in to see him, and to arrange to go out walking or bicycling, at least twice a week. He would talk about the sort of matters he thought would be of interest and would invite him to his rooms to meet men in whom he would be interested. Indeed it was at that time and under those circumstances that Mr. Benson first met Rupert Brooke, of whom Mallory was then seeing a good deal.

Mr. Benson has assured me that sometimes while out walking with Mallory he used to pour out lamentations over his own unhappy condition—it is almost impossible for a man in that state of mind not to do so. He felt that he could neither read nor write, and it did not seem possible that the cloud would ever lift. Mallory began by trying to laugh it all away and to banter him, to assure him that he was still an interesting companion and that it was obvious to all their friends that he was getting better. But he persisted, and Mallory finally begged him, with a look full of confused pain, for both their sakes not to indulge in these miserable and distorted reveries.

It must have been a great strain to listen to this morbid outpouring from one so much older, whom he had previously known as a good-humoured and easy-going companion; and it is, I think, a remarkable tribute to Mallory's loyalty and goodness that at a time when his own mind was expanding in the company of many of the most interesting young men of the day, when the days seemed hardly long enough for all that he wanted to say and hear, to read and do, he continued week after week to frequent the company of a man old enough to be his father, who was plunged in solitary gloom, often hardly able to sustain conversation at all—and to do all this as if it were for his own pleasure rather than for the consolation of the other. To illustrate how he did this Mr. Benson recounted to me the sort of conversation which frequently took place. Mallory would look into his room, soon after two o'clock, and find him plunged in a sort of melancholy stupor after the effort of a morning's teaching.

'Shall we go out?'

'No, I think I won't go out this afternoon—you don't mind, do you? I shall go out a little later. Besides I am not fit company for the young and gay.'

'What nonsense! besides it is our regular day for going out—and I want to talk to you particularly, I have got stuck in an essay, and can't turn the corner.'

'Very well!' rising with an air of sullen resignation.

'Oh, don't come if you really don't feel up to it—but you always get better out walking, you know.'

'Well, you mustn't let me talk about myself.'

'You won't have the chance—I have half a dozen things to tell you. You are the only person who really appreciates my experiences.'

With such a graceful turn he would present the coming walk as a concession to himself and lift, so to speak, the load of egoism from the invalid by exhibiting it upon his own shoulders.

GEORGE LEIGH-MALLORY

And in the evening, sometimes, it would be the same. Knowing that his friend would probably feel incapable of reading and unwilling to invite any one to his rooms, Mallory would appear, uninvited, about nine o'clock.

'What about a game of picquet?' he would say, 'I have been arguing with half a dozen people. They are so stupid, and then I am rude.'

'Only intellectually rude.'

'Yes, of course, but I want a game to calm me down.'

There were several good walks with him which I can recall myself, in the Cambridgeshire country, for although it was to the hills that his eyes were constantly turned Mallory enjoyed, too, the wide open spaces of the fens. One long day we spent on the river at St. Ives. We rowed up a much reed-grown channel to Houghton, and watched a huge dripping mill-wheel, with the sweet scent of the fresh river water all about it. Then we took the other arm of the river, and by dint of carrying the boat round a deserted lock, got to Hemingford Grey and Hemingford Abbots, two quiet villages with fine churches close to the river, and a view over the wide alluvial plain of the Ouse. Other days were spent, more energetically, afoot, tracing the prehistoric earthworks with which the uplands toward Newmarket abound, or following the whole course of the *Via Devana* where it flings away, a green and crinkly riband over the Gog Magog hills, straight to some forgotten goal.

Although he was just then beginning his experi-

CAMBRIDGE DAYS

ences among the mountains at home, and it was two years or more since he had first been to the Alps, yet so little was he inclined to speak of his own unique prowess that there were many among his undergraduate friends who were hardly conscious of these activities of the vacations. It is astonishing to me, looking back, to think how little he can have talked about climbing. I had not then begun any serious association with the mountains, and although I definitely wanted to climb, and wanted to get into touch with some one who would tell me where to go and what to do, yet it must have been a year or more after I first made friends with him that I became aware of the part the mountains played in Mallory's life.

How profound a part that was I must now endeavour, with his own help, to show.

III

THE MOUNTAINEER

THE devotion of the mountaineer to his pursuit is a phenomenon which has to be accepted, for it cannot be argued about. Justifiable or unjustifiable?—An inspiration or an insane risk of life?—each man must choose his view according to his temperament.

'Man should not dispute nor assert, but whisper results to his neighbour'; and although it is perhaps a vain thing even to whisper one's beliefs, yet, when a life so full of promise as George Mallory's, and so charged with gifts which make for a full and effective span of years on earth, is lost in an attempt to get to the top of a mountain—even the highest in the world—it seems inevitable that one should try to make clear what the mountains meant to him; and why, and in what sense, he could himself have regarded his own death as a fulfilment and not a senseless waste.

Happily we have the pith of the matter in his own words: so well done, as it seems to me, that I shall quote the article at length with only occasional omissions.

'I seem to distinguish two sorts of climber', he writes,[1] 'those who take a high line about climbing and those who take no particular line at all. . . .

[1] 'The Mountaineer as Artist', *Climbers' Club Journal*, 1914, p. 28.

THE MOUNTAINEER

Climbing for them [i. e. the first sort] means something more than a common amusement, and more than other forms of athletic pursuit mean to other men; it has a recognized importance in life. If you could deprive them of it they would be conscious of a definite degradation, a loss of virtue. They have an arrogance with regard to this hobby never equalled. . . . It never, for instance, presents itself to them as comparable with field sports. They assume an unmeasured superiority. And yet—they give no explanation. . . .

'Climbers who, like myself, take the high line have much to explain, and it is time they set about it. Notoriously they endanger their lives. With what object? If only for some physical pleasure, to enjoy certain movements of the body and to experience the zest of emulation, then it is not worth while. Climbers are only a particularly foolish set of desperadoes; they are on the same plane with hunters, and many degrees less reasonable. The only defence for mountaineering puts it on a higher plane than mere physical sensation. It is asserted that the climber experiences higher emotions; he gets some good for his soul. His opponent may well feel sceptical about this argument. He, too, may claim to consider his soul's good when he can take a holiday. Probably it is true of any one who spends a well-earned fortnight in healthy enjoyment at the seaside that he comes back a better, that is to say a more virtuous, man than he went. How are the climber's joys worth more than the seaside? What are these higher emotions to which he refers so elusively? And if they really are so valuable, is there no safer way of reaching them? Do mountaineers consider these questions and answer them again and again from fresh experience, or are they content with some magic certainty born of comparative ignorance long ago?

'It would be a wholesome tonic, perhaps, more often to meet an adversary who argued on these lines. In practice I find that few men ever want to discuss mountaineering seriously. I suppose they imagine that a discussion with me would be unprofitable; and I must confess that if any one does open the question my impulse is to put him off. I can assume a vague disdain for civilization, and I can make phrases about beautiful surroundings, and puff them out, as one who has a secret and does not care to reveal it because no one would understand—phrases which refer to the divine riot of Nature in her ecstasy of making mountains.

'Thus I appeal to the effect of mountain scenery upon my aesthetic sensibility. But, even if I can communicate by words a true feeling, I have explained nothing. Aesthetic delight is vitally connected with our performance, but it neither explains nor excuses it. No one for a moment dreams that our apparently wilful proceedings are determined merely by our desire to see what is beautiful. The mountain railway could cater for such desires. By providing viewpoints at a number of stations, and by concealing all signs of its own mechanism, it might be so completely organized that all the aesthetic joys of the mountaineer should be offered to its intrepid ticketholders. It would achieve this object with a comparatively small expenditure of time, and would even have, one might suppose, a decisive advantage by affording to all lovers of the mountains the opportunity of sharing their emotions with a large and varied multitude of their fellow-men. And yet the idea of associating this mechanism with a snow mountain is the abomination of every species of mountaineer. To him it appears as a kind of rape. The fact that he so regards it indicates the emphasis with which he rejects the crude aesthetic reasons as his central defence.

'I suppose that, in the opinion of many people who have opportunities of judging, mountaineers have no ground for claiming for their pursuit a superiority as regards the natural beauties that attend it. And certainly many huntsmen would resent their making any such claim. We cannot, therefore, remove mountaineering from the plane of hunting by a composite representation of its merits—by asserting that physical and aesthetic joys are blent for us and not for others.

'Nevertheless, I am still arrogant, and still confident in the superiority of mountaineering over all other forms of recreation. But what do I mean by this superiority? And in what measure do I claim it? On what level do we place mountaineering? What place in the whole order of experience is occupied by our experience as mountaineers? The answer to these questions must be very nearly connected with the whole explanation of our position; it may actually be found to include in itself a defence of mountaineering.

GEORGE LEIGH-MALLORY

'It must be admitted at the outset that our periodic literature gives little indication that our performance is concerned no less with the spiritual side of us than with the physical. This is, in part, because we require certain practical information of any one who describes an expedition. Our journals, with one exception, do not pretend to be elevated literature, but aim only at providing useful knowledge for climbers. With this purpose we try to show exactly where upon a mountain our course lay, in what manner the conditions of snow and ice and rocks and weather were or were not favourable to our enterprise, and what were the actual difficulties we had to overcome and the dangers we had to meet. Naturally, if we accept these circumstances, the impulse for literary expression vanishes; not so much because the matter is not suitable as because, for literary expression, it is too difficult to handle. A big expedition in the Alps, say a traverse of Mont Blanc, would be a superb theme for an epic poem. But we are not all even poets, still less Homers or Miltons. We do, indeed, possess lyric poetry that is concerned with mountains, and value it highly for the expression of much that we feel about them. But little of it can be said to suggest that mountaineering in the technical sense offers an emotional experience which cannot otherwise be reached. A few essays and a few descriptions do give some indication that the spiritual part of man is concerned. Most of those who describe expeditions do not even treat them as adventure, still less as being connected with any emotional experience peculiar to mountaineering. . . .

THE MOUNTAINEER

' These observations about our mountain literature are not made by way of censure or in disappointment; they are put forward as phenomena, which have to be explained, not so much by the nature of mountaineers, but rather by the nature of their performance. The explanation which commends itself to me is derived very simply from the conception of mountaineering, which, expressed or unexpressed, is common, I imagine, to all us of the arrogant sort. We do not think that our aesthetic experiences of sunrises and sunsets and clouds and thunder are supremely important facts in mountaineering, but rather that they cannot thus be separated and catalogued and described individually as experiences at all. They are not incidental in mountaineering, but a vital and inseparable part of it; they are not ornamental, but structural; they are not various items causing emotion but parts of an emotional whole; they are the crystal pools perhaps, but they owe their life to a continuous stream.

' It is this unity that makes so many attempts to describe aesthetic detail seem futile. Somehow they miss the point and fail to touch us. It is because they are only fragments. If we take one moment and present its emotional quality apart from the whole, it has lost the very essence that gave it a value. If we write about an expedition from the emotional point of view in any part of it, we ought so to write about the whole adventure from beginning to end.

' A day well spent in the Alps is like some great symphony. Andante, andantissimo sometimes, is the first movement—the grim, sickening plod up the moraine. But how forgotten when the blue light of dawn flickers over the hard, clean snow! The new *motif* is ushered in, as it were, very gently on the lesser wind instruments, hautboys, and flutes, remote but melodious and infinitely hopeful, caught by the violins in the growing light, and torn out by all the bows with quivering chords as the summits, one by one, are enmeshed in the gold web of day, till at last the whole band, in triumphant accord, has seized the air and romps in magnificent frolic, because there you are at last marching, all a-tingle with warm blood, under the sun. And so throughout the day successive moods induce the symphonic whole—allegro while you break the back of an expedition and the issue is still in doubt; scherzo, perhaps, as you leap up the final rocks of the arête or cut steps in a last short slope, with the ice-chips dancing and swimming and bubbling and bounding with magic gaiety over the crisp surface in their mad glissade; and then, for the descent, sometimes again andante, because, while the summit was still to win, you forgot that the business of descending may be serious and long; but in the end scherzo once more—with the brakes on for sunset.

' Expeditions in the Alps are all different, no less than symphonies are different, and each is a fresh experience. Not all are equally buoyant with hope and strength; nor is it only the proportion of grim to pleasant that varies, but no less the quality of these and other ingredients and the manner of their mixing. But every mountain adventure is emotionally complete. The spirit goes on a journey just as does the body, and this journey has a beginning and an end, and is concerned with all that happens between these extremities. You cannot say that one part of your adventure was emotional while another was not, any more than you can say of your journey that one part was travelling and another was not. You cannot subtract parts and still have the whole. Each part depends for its value upon all the other parts, and the manner in which it is related to them. The glory of sunrise in the Alps is not independent of what has passed and what is to come; without the day that is dying and the night that is to come the reverie of sunset would be less suggestive, and the deep valley-lights would lose their promise of repose. Still more, the ecstasy of the summit is conditioned by the events of getting up and the prospects of getting down.

'Mountain scenes occupy the same place in our consciousness with remembered melody. It is all one whether I find myself humming the air of some great symphonic movement or gazing upon some particular configuration of rock and snow, or peak and glacier, or even more humbly upon some colour harmony of meadow and sweet pinewood in Alpine valley. Impressions of things seen return unbidden to the mind, so that we seem to have whole series of places where we love to spend idle moments, inns, as it were, inviting us by the roadside, and many of them pleasant and comfortable Gorphwysfas, so well known to us by now that we make the journey easily enough with a homing instinct, and never feel a shock of surprise, however remote they seem, when we find ourselves there. Many people, it appears, have strange dreamlands, where they are accustomed to wander at ease, where no 'dull brain perplexes and retards', nor tired body and heavy limbs, but where the whole emotional being flows, unrestrained and unencumbered, it knows not whither, like a stream rippling happily in its clean sandy bed, careless towards the infinite. My own experience has more of the earth. My mental homes are real places, distinctly seen and not hard to recognize. Only a little while ago, when a sentence I was writing got into a terrible tangle, I visited one of them. An infant river meanders coolly in a broad, grassy valley; it winds along as gently almost as some glassy snake of the plains, for the valley is so flat that its slope is imperceptible. The green hills on either side are smooth and pleasing to the eye, and eventually close in, though not completely. Here the stream plunges down a steep and craggy hillside far into the shadow of a deeper valley. You may follow it down by a rough path, and then, turning aside, before you quite reach the bottom of the second valley, along a grassy ledge, you may find a modest inn. The scene was visited in reality by three tired walkers at the end of a first day in the Alps a few seasons back. It is highly agreeable. When I discover myself looking again upon the features of this landscape, I walk no longer in a vain shadow, disquieting myself, but a delicious serenity embraces my whole being. In another scene which I still sometimes visit, though not so often as formerly, the main feature is a number of uniform truncated cones with a circular base of, perhaps, eight inches diameter; they are made of reddish sand. They were, in fact, made long ago by filling a flower-pot with sandy soil from the country garden where I spent a considerable part of my childhood. The emotional quality of this scene is more exciting than that of the other. It recalls the first occasion upon which I made sand-pies, and something of the creative force of that moment is associated with the tidy little heaps of reddish sand.

'For any ardent mountaineer whose imaginative parts are made like mine, normally, as I should say, the mountains will naturally supply a large part of this hinterland, and the more important scenes will probably be mountainous—an indication in itself that the mountain experiences, unless they are merely terrible, are particularly valuable.

'It is difficult to see why certain moments should have this queer vitality, as though the mind's home contained some mystic cavern set with gems which wait only for a gleam of light to reveal their hidden glory. What principle is it that determines this vitality? Perhaps the analogy with musical experience may still suffice. Mountain scenes appear to recur, not only in the same quality with tunes from a great work, say, Mozart or Beethoven, but from the same differentiating cause. It is not mere intensity of feeling that determines the places of tunes in my subconscious self, but chiefly some other principle. When the chords of melody are split, and unsatisfied suggestions of complete harmony are tossed among the instruments; when the firm rhythm is lost in remote pools and eddies, the mind roams perplexed; it experiences remorse and associates it with no cause; grief, and it names no sad event; desires crying aloud and unfulfilled, and yet it will not formulate the object of them; but when the great tide of music rises with a resolved purpose, floating the strewn wreckage and bearing it up together in its embracing stream, like a supreme spirit in the glorious act of creation, then the vague distresses and cravings are satisfied, a divine completeness of harmony possesses all the senses and the mind as though the universe and the individual were in exact accord, pursuing a common aim with the efficiency of mechanical perfection. Similarly, some parts of a climbing day give us the feeling of things unfulfilled; we doubt and tremble; we go forward not as men determined to reach a fixed goal; our plans do not convince us and miscarry; discomforts are not willingly accepted as a proper necessity; spirit and body seem to betray each other: but a time comes when all this is changed and we experience a harmony and a satisfaction. The individual is in a sense submerged, yet not so as to be less conscious; rather his consciousness is specially alert, and he comes to a finer realization of himself than ever before. It is these moments of supremely harmonious experience that remain always with us and part of us.

'But once again. What is the value of our emotional experience among mountains? We may show by comparison the kind of feeling we have, but might not that comparison be applied with a similar result in other spheres?

THE MOUNTAINEER

'... The fact that sportsmen are, with regard to their sport, highly emotional beings is at once so strange and so true that a lifetime might well be spent in the testing of it. ... The elation of sportsmen in success, their depression in failure, their long-spun vivacity in anecdote—these are the great tests, and by their quality may be seen the elemental play of emotions among all kinds of sportsmen. ... Sport is for sportsmen a part of their emotional experience, as mountaineering is for mountaineers. How, then, shall we distinguish emotionally between the mountaineer and the sportsman?

'The great majority of men are in a sense artists; some are active and creative, and some participate passively. No doubt those who create differ in some way fundamentally from those who do not create; but they hold this artistic impulse in common: all alike desire expression for the emotional side of their nature. The behaviour of those who are devoted to the higher forms of Art shows this clearly enough. It is clearest of all, perhaps, in the drama, in dancing, and in music. Not only those who perform are artists, but also those who are moved by the performance. Artists, in this sense, are not distinguished by the power of expressing emotion, but the power of feeling that emotional experience out of which Art is made. ... Arrogant mountaineers are all artists, independently of any other consideration, because they cultivate emotional experience for its own sake; and so for the same reason are sportsmen. It is not paradoxical to assert that all sportsmen —real sportsmen, I mean—are artists; it is merely to apply that term logically, as it ought to be applied. A large part of the human race is covered in this way by an epithet usually vague and specialized, and so it ought to be. No difference in kind divides the individual who is commonly said to be artistic from the sportsman who is supposed not so to be. On the contrary, the sportsman is a recognizable kind of artist. So soon as pleasure is being pursued, not simply for its face value, not in the simplest way, but for some more remote and emotional object, it partakes of the nature of Art. . . .

'But there is Art and ART. We may distinguish amongst artists. Without an exact classification or order of merit we do so distinguish habitually. The 'Fine Arts' are called 'fine' presumably because we consider that all Arts are not fine. The epithet artistic is commonly limited to those who are seen to have the artistic sense developed in a peculiar degree.

'It is precisely in making these distinctions that we may estimate what we set out to determine—the value of mountaineering in the whole order of our emotional experience. To what part of the artistic sense of man does mountaineering belong? To the part that causes him to be moved by music or painting, or to the part that makes him enjoy a game?

'By putting the question in this form we perceive at once the gulf that divides the arrogant mountaineer from the sportsman. It seemed perfectly natural to compare a day in the Alps with a symphony. For mountaineers of my sort mountaineering is rightfully so comparable; but no sportsman could or would make the same claim for cricket or hunting, or whatever his particular sport might be. He recognizes the existence of the sublime in great Art, and knows, even if he cannot feel, that its manner of stirring the heart is altogether different and vaster. But mountaineers do not admit this difference in the emotional plane of mountaineering and Art. They claim that something sublime is the essence of mountaineering. They can compare the call of the hills to the melody of wonderful music, and the comparison is not ridiculous.'

To say that mountaineering was to Mallory a spiritual necessity will not sound extravagant, I hope, after this confession of his faith, even to the most determined dweller in the plains. Reading it, one feels that mountains had done for him what they do for every one who begins to surrender to them: they had transformed his scale of values and coloured his attitude to everything else. Mountaineering had become a religion. It demanded, as he saw it, the exercise of moral qualities, patience, and self-control, and sometimes fortitude, and the subordination of all else to the striving towards an end greater than himself. And it had, like other religions, its moments of ecstasy, of worship, and of abasement. It went further: it seemed essential to him to carry back into everyday life the illumination found, as it were, before the altar: to live all the time in the spirit in which he set out for and carried through a climb: not to be found unworthy of the mountains, which had given so much, in any activity or in any particular.

GEORGE LEIGH-MALLORY

It was always among the mountains that one saw his fiery energy at its hottest, his judgement at its coolest and most collected. Because he was there most happy, it was always among mountains that one saw him most serene, most thoughtful for others, most constantly good tempered. It was as though the approach to this art of mountaineering, this high spiritual endeavour, was only to be made with a mind exalted above pettiness and irritation. If deprived of it he would have felt, in his own words, 'a definite degradation, a loss of virtue'; and so each summer, when opportunity and funds allowed, found him in the Alps, and between whiles he would seek virtue among the mountains of Wales or Cumberland.

For the most part, of course, mountaineering in this country cannot reproduce, even remotely, the experience of an Alpine day. The variety is of another order: in the technique of the climbing no less than in the face of nature, dawn and sunset, fair weather and foul, colour and shadowy rock; so that it would be an unfair compression of the symphonic simile to harness it also to climbing days at home. And yet in this different medium the same effects are achieved as by wider ranging adventures. The virtue is there, to be won by him who seeks it aright among the rock faces of our British hills. The harmony is more secret perhaps, more subjective, less built upon nature's motifs, a harmony of hand and brain known only to the arrogant mountaineer.

For success in a game the body relies not upon intelligence but upon instinct, upon the lightning partnership of eye and limb; while walking, the intelligence is lulled asleep and the mind soothed by impressions of outward beauty; but on a rock-climb the body and brain go out hand-in-hand to an adventure. I believe that is one of the secrets: that in no other pursuit are alertness and firmness of muscle so united under the control of intelligence. On difficult rocks there is hardly a faculty which is not called upon for the solution of the problem ahead: quickness of eye and a sensitive touch in the hands and feet, every muscle of the body performing its part in the maintenance of a balanced poise, and, most important of all, intelligent judgement served by quick observation and past experience. All are focused upon an aim which is for the moment supreme: the deliberate and certain, although rapid, movement which leads, after moments of high nervous tension, to the luxurious ease of complete security.

In all the technique of this movement upon steep rocks, Mallory became early an acknowledged master. He had not a particularly long reach, but the perfection of his balance and the great strength of his arms and fingers enabled him to make confident use of every inch that he possessed, and to move with a sort of large rhythmical ease which was very deceptive when one came to try and follow him. He was an ideal leader, for besides the skill with which each difficult move was surmounted and the complete confidence it gave to those behind, he had a way of making one conscious of the great reserve of endurance which he had at call, and at the same time that he was constantly though unobtrusively observant of the form shown by other members of his party.

To strangers unaccustomed to his performances it is true that a first day under his leadership was sometimes an experience rather too highly charged with emotion. At Easter 1911 there was among the party collected at the Pen-y-Pass Hotel the Austrian climber, Dr. Blodig, who had climbed all the 'four thousand metre' peaks in the Alps except four. As the guest of the Climbers' Club he was being shown what Wales could provide to compare with his native Alps. On Easter Sunday Lliwedd was explored under the guidance of George Mallory, and on his return the Herr Doctor announced with many shakes of the head that 'that young man will not be alive for long'. Poor Mallory was quite upset. He always used to defend himself vigorously against any suggestion that he was not a perfectly prudent mountaineer and looked most comically dismayed and surprised over this dictum. He *was* prudent, according to his own standards; but his standards were not those of the ordinary medium-good rock climber. The fact was that difficult rocks had become to him a perfectly normal element; his reach, his strength, and his admirable technique, joined to a sort of cat-like agility, made him feel completely secure on rocks so difficult as to fill less competent climbers with a sense of hazardous enterprise. But he was very careful of unskilled performers, and very down on any clumsiness or carelessness. I never saw him do a reckless or an ill-considered thing on steep rocks. He hated the irresponsible folly and ignorance which led incompetent people into dangerous situations, and so brought mountaineering into disrepute. On this occasion in Wales he helped to rescue, on Easter Monday, a stranger from Bradford who was making a new route of his own up some wet mossy slabs on Clogwyn-y-Person in shoes and a long mackintosh. The wretched man, as soon as he found himself in safety, offered his rescuers a sovereign, and the whole episode produced endless mirth; but Mallory was too indignant really to enjoy even the sovereign.

He took risks, of course, especially when alone. He climbed alone more than was customary, and such adventures as his solitary invention of the Slab Climb on the East Buttress of Lliwedd, already mentioned, got him more of a reputation for recklessness than he really deserved. But young men of twenty-one are apt to take risks, and risks are to some extent inherent in mountaineering. He was adventurous; he admitted it freely; he was made that way. This was one reason why he was so fond of solitary climbing; it so heightened the sense of adventure, and when alone he took risks for no one but himself, as he would explain if hard pressed. But he saw a clear distinction between the love of adventure, the pitting of a man's skill and strength and knowledge against difficulties and odds, and the love of danger for its own sake. The one was his delight—with the other he had no patience. I remember his scathing comments on one or two climbing accidents where the parties were obviously tackling ascents entirely beyond their powers, or where there had been admitted carelessness in the matter of precautions, such as belaying or using unsound rope. ' They had no *business* to be there! ' he said in tones of angry grief, about one of these accidents.

Mallory's early reputation was made almost wholly as a rock climber, for after his first two seasons of guideless climbing with R. L. G. Irving, 1904 and 1905, he had to wait four years before he again saw the Alps, this time in the company of Geoffrey Young. During this season of 1909 their climbs were done some of them with, and some without, professional guides. Of the latter the most remarkable was their first ascent, with Donald Robertson, of the great south-east ridge of the Nesthorn, direct from Belalp over the top of the Unterbachhorn. There is a fascinating account of this climb, by Geoffrey Young, written in retrospect after ten years.[1] The rocks were badly iced, and the party of three did not reach the summit until seven p.m., after twelve hours of almost continuous climbing since their start up the rocks of the Unterbachhorn. It was on this climb that Mallory had, so far as I know, his only serious tumble. The story is worth telling. It was past six o'clock, and they found themselves at last at the foot of the dark tower which showed as the last great obstacle on the ridge. On each side, to south and north, the walls of the ridge rushed down into nothingness. Above, the fluted crags looked practicable for some ten feet, but after a further ten all view was cut off by a cornice of ice

[1] *Climbers' Club Journal*, 1920.

On the Moine ridge of the Aiguille Verte, 1909

and rock above their heads. Mallory took the lead, and traversed out from their rock-shelf across the rib and hollow of the south face, seeking a way upwards; Young meanwhile passing the rope over a small but sound nick on the slab at his shoulder. From this point Geoffrey Young shall tell the story himself. 'He disappeared behind a further volute. I could hear him, but the rope ceased to run out. The minutes passed. He was trying for some possible line up the smooth flutings, clinging to the wall, and with the overhang above checking each attempt. The long continued effort must have been exhausting, for the holds over all this wall were few and inadequate, up to the level at which they ceased altogether. It was a relief to see him returning into sight, swinging agilely across the cliff on a broken line of finger-holds. But, unexpectedly, when he reached the scoop between the two nearest upright slats, about ten feet away from me, I saw him glance upward, pause, and then begin to wrestle up it. The sight of my shelf, recalling our dangerous alternative route up the north face, may have suggested to him a last attempt on the south wall as a preferable course. So far as I could see, he had no real holds at all; but he fought his way up magnificently, until all that remained below the rock cornice, which cut off everything else above from my sight, were his two boots. These were clinging, cat-like, and continued to cling for long seconds, to almost imperceptible irregularities on the walls of the rift. The mere sight of them made me breathless; and I tightened every muscle, ready to 'spring' the rope on its nick. For, on such foothold no climber would choose to wait long, were his hand-holds adequate for a lift; and if George's hand-holds were *not* adequate . . .! Any way, they did not serve for the gymnastic backward swing, outward and upward, which he was forced to risk. I saw the boots flash from the wall without even a scrape; and, equally soundlessly, a grey streak flickered downward, and past me, and out of sight. So much did the wall, to which he had clung so long, overhang that from the instant he lost hold he touched nothing until the rope stopped him in mid-air over the glacier, out of sight. I had had time to think, as I flung my body forward on to the belayed rope, grinding it and my hands against the slab, that no rope could stand such a jerk; and even to think out what our next action must be—so instantaneous is thought. The boots had been standing some fifteen to twenty feet above me, so that the clear fall could not have been much less than forty feet. But the rope held, springing like an elastic band, and cracking under my chest and hands on the rock. . . . At first there was nothing to do but hold on, and watch the pendulum movement of a tense cord straining over the edge and down into space. My first cautious shouts were unanswered. Then there came, from nowhere, a tranquil call to let out more rope, and to 'lower away'. So soon as I was convinced that, owing to the good fortune of a clear fall, he had not even been hurt, I complied. The short visible length of rope slackened, and then began to jerk along the edge of the shelf on which I stood. George had spied a line of possible holds across the face of the cliff below him. As I lowered him on the rope, he coolly hooked himself in to them with his axe, and proceeded to make his way along the invisible cliff underneath me. Presently he appeared up a slanting groove, and rejoined me on the mantelshelf, apparently entirely undisturbed. He had not even let go of his axe during the fall. The whole incident had passed so swiftly and unemotionally—I had almost said with such decorum—that Donald, twenty feet below us, and round the corner on the north face, remained unaware that anything unusual had happened. Nor did we enlighten him at the time.'

'He had not even let go of his axe during the fall!' That, to the mountaineer, is the most eloquent touch of all.

The next year, 1910, Mallory again managed to get to the Alps, but with what a different scope for his activities! I should say it was the most trying season ever spent in the Alps by a man of his temperament. He had brought out with him a boy of fifteen and a half or so—in his own phrase, 'bear-leading'. The idea, approved by the boy's parents, was that he should be taught and encouraged to climb. But he had no taste whatever for the pursuit; he was weak and clumsy, he disliked cold and exertion, and it was impossible to kindle in him the smallest spark of enthusiasm. He opposed the whole mass of his *vis inertiae* to Mallory's efforts to induce him to undertake even the most modest of expeditions. A mutual friend who met them both at Zermatt has told me that Mallory's consternation and astonishment at this state of affairs were pitiable to witness. He had already begun to set the feet of those younger than himself on mountain paths at home with some success, and he simply did not know what to make of this pupil. One of the things which always irritated him most was any failure to respond to stimulus—a ' jelly-fish ' attitude. His own enthusiasm was so tremendous—not only for mountaineering, it was a quality of itself in him—and capable of such sustained effort, he was so ready to throw anything and everything into its service, that he found it harder than most people to make allowance for apathy. He was irritated and depressed when he turned up at Zermatt; and he behaved extraordinarily well. The contrast between the last season, when all his energy and enthusiasm were finding a vent in big expeditions with Geoffrey Young, and this, when he was tied by the leg to a fifteen-year old, whom he could neither abandon nor drag up the mountains with him, must have been overwhelmingly present to his mind, but those who met him never once saw him fail for a moment in duty or temper towards his charge. He used to persuade, cajole, and rag him with good-tempered irony, but he stuck to his job with a fine conscientiousness. It would not be true to say that he accepted the situation, because it was a situation which he would have thought it wrong to accept—a boy who had the chance to climb and wouldn't! And he made no sort of secret, to others, of his irritation. But to the boy himself his patience and good temper were unfailing, and all the more remarkable at his age, and in him.

THE MOUNTAINEER

It is probably from the summer of 1911—that most wonderful of seasons when for weeks on end the weather seemed as if it *could not* break—that we should date Mallory's evolution as a fully qualified mountaineer among the High Alps. Of his four previous seasons, although the first two, with R. L. G. Irving, had been guideless, he would then have been too much of a novice to take much part in the counsels of the party; and during the two latter he had climbed for the most part with guides. In 1911 he was again without guides and again in the company of R. L. G. Irving and H. E. G. Tyndale, and although he seems to have taken but little part in the actual leading, he did share in the deliberations and planning of the expeditions. So it is fair to say that in this season he first began to taste, in the Alps, the full flavour of big climbs undertaken without professional assistance. No one without climbing experience can realize how greatly this one circumstance alters the character of an expedition. All the technical problems involved, such as time, weather, route, practicability of obstacles, and so on, take on a sudden fresh importance and become immensely more interesting and exciting; and more than this, the whole psychological quality of the experience is changed. Every climber knows how, at first, at any rate, the mere fact of being first man on the rope intensifies all the experiences of any given climb: each impression, whether of difficulty or certainty or danger or security, comes with a sharp clear impact on his consciousness, and his reactions to each are intensified in proportion. Among a party thrown entirely on its own resources for the undertaking of first-class expeditions in the Alps, both the interest of the staff work and this heightened psychological experience are present in the highest degree.

Mallory was deeply interested in both these sides of mountaineering. The psychological side was to him of the first importance; but the staff work absorbed him too. He got intense enjoyment from the work of planning an expedition, studying the routes beforehand either on the spot, or from maps and photographs, and working out with detailed care and much ingenuity how it was to be tackled. He had, too, a rare and great gift for this particular and rather technical side of leadership, as became apparent later in his life. He had an extremely quick eye for a mountain, picking up very rapidly the smallest indication of a possible route; and his memory, bad for some things, was almost perfect for this. He could carry in his head, in bulk and in detail, the whole structure of some peak, or mountain wall in which he hoped to effect a breach; and he used to work on them in his mind at odd times, much as a chess-player is said to work out chess problems in his bath. In winter, when the Alps seemed very far away, Mallory would suddenly come out of a brown study and break irrelevantly into a pause in some conversation with a question, ' what do you think about this? '—and then would follow a project for some new route over a mountain, a col, a never-attempted ridge, or some unfrequented face. Mont Blanc and the Matterhorn attracted him especially. Most of his ' wild chimaeras ' related to one or the other. He was always drawn to the big and the unexplored—the great walls that mountaineers as a rule set aside as obviously impossible. The south-east face of the Matterhorn, the south face of Mont Blanc, between the Brouillard Ridge and the Aiguille Blanche de Peûteret, and the large eastern cliffs of Mont Blanc between the Peûteret Ridge and the Col de la Brenva—over all these his climbing fancy brooded, year after year, questioning, speculating, pondering the possibilities. And while he climbed in their neighbourhood his eye was always on the watch for some fresh clue or hint that might give away the secret of their invincibility.

One soon learns to accept with philosophic resignation all vagaries of weather in the Alps; but I shall never be able quite to forgive those thunderstorms of 1920, recurring every three days, while we shivered and hoped at the Gamba hut on the south side of Mont Blanc. I like to think that but for them one of these long cherished dreams would have been accomplished: to find a way up the south face of Mont Blanc from the Col du Fresnay. For we had gone to the Gamba for that purpose, but the weather never allowed us to get higher than the top of the *Innominata* and to plan our prospective bivouac and route on the vast wall above. And then, next year, while Mallory was making the first exploration of Everest, the climb was accomplished. The great south face was climbed by G. F. Gugliermina from the Col du Fresnay, and the route of the successful party was almost precisely that picked out and prospected by the keen eye and judgement of George Mallory the year before.

As a background to this observation and planning of future climbs there was always, as I have said, his preoccupation with the psychological aspect. Almost all his writing about mountains or climbing is coloured by this question of the value of the mountaineer's experience. In the 'Mountaineer as artist' he has given us, vividly enough, his conception of the peculiar quality of mountaineering as an emotional experience. And this was no magazine article written to satisfy the demands of an editor: to Mallory the whole matter of a man's reaction to the mountains was intensely real and important; he returned to it again and again, and even during the war, when the Alps were for years out of reach, it was a subject to which he naturally turned as a refuge.

When he returned from his season in 1911 it was clear there had been one expedition which stood out for him above all others in this respect. His party had made the traverse of Mont Blanc by the eastern buttress of Mont Maudit. He had been unwell during the earlier part of the climb, and I remember listening as he tried to explain how, gradually, the impressions from without had entered and overcome, bit by bit, the disastrous and defeating emotions which illness and weakness on a mountain produce, till the question of comfort or discomfort ceased to absorb his attention, and he was free, as he said, from himself. In that freedom, moving among some of the noblest sights of the Alps, he learnt something new about the meaning of mountains. He had got

THE MOUNTAINEER

hold of some further experience which had affected him powerfully. It is probably impossible to communicate such experiences, though the fact and effect of them may be evident, but to Mallory they were the most important things in mountaineering. He wanted to understand them, to realize their meaning and place in the many-sided whole that makes up mountaineering experience, and to discover their bearing on the rest of life. It is not a subject which lends itself to precise expression, and he was frankly bothered by the vagueness which seemed unavoidable in any account of it; but this effort to understand became a constant preoccupation with him. Valuing these experiences highly, he desired to be increasingly aware of and responsive to them, and much of his time on mountains and off them was spent in studying the conditions in himself and in others which were most favourable to awareness and to response. The value of an expedition, for him, lay very largely in the extent to which it promoted such experiences, whether by beauty or difficulty or variety or surprise, and in just that measure of freedom, of ready awareness and response, that he found in himself. Sometimes the mountains did not do their share, were ugly or repellent, and then he almost hated them. Sometimes he was not able to respond, and then he almost hated himself. ' I was *heavy*! ' he used to say in tones of deep disgust.

He made an attempt, five years later during idle days in a dug-out, to give an account of the Mont Blanc climb seen in retrospect ' from inside, not from outside', in terms of sensations and emotions rather than of facts. He achieved his end as far, perhaps, as it could be achieved. . . . 'How to get the best of it all? One must conquer, achieve, get to the top; one must know the end to be convinced that one can win the end—to know there's no dream that mustn't be dared. . . . Is this the summit, crowning the day? How cool and quiet! We're not exultant; but delighted, joyful, soberly astonished. . . . Have we vanquished an enemy? None but ourselves. Have we gained success? That word means nothing here. Have we won a kingdom? No . . . and yes. We have achieved an ultimate satisfaction . . . fulfilled a destiny. . . . To struggle and to understand—never this last without the other; such is the law. . . .'[1]

The value of his attempt, like the value of the musical simile, lay for Mallory in the effort to get clear for himself the quality and importance of the climber's experience. He was constantly regretting that so few mountaineering writers ever attempted this. 'They go on telling us where they have been, and what they did—why won't they tell us what they thought about it? That might have some interest.'

Of the success of his own attempt opinions will differ, but the article remains, at any rate, as a novel and interesting experiment in Alpine literature.

[1] *Alpine Journal*, vol. xxxii, p. 162.

IV

CHARTERHOUSE

MOUNTAINS have led us on some years beyond Cambridge days and we must now return to the year there which followed George Mallory's degree. I do not remember that during his fourth year he was pursuing any very definite course of study. He was interested in certain aspects of History, more especially in the biographical and social side, and about this time he set to work upon a study of James Boswell. In the form of an essay it was sent in for the Burney Prize and although unsuccessful it was honourably mentioned and Mallory was encouraged to expand it with a view to publication in book form. The further work upon it was much interrupted by his going abroad for six months, so that it was not until a year or so later that the book was published. Although perhaps a little ponderous in style, with sentences too elaborate, the book may be read with a good deal of interest. Indeed, it may be said that Mallory was one of the first to treat Johnson's biographer as in himself a figure of real literary interest, as an incomparable dramatist and stylist who deliberately worked up his materials, and to rescue him from contemptuous dismissal as an ass whose industrious toadying had, in spite of himself, enabled him to produce a good biography. A writer on Boswell must face a psychological enigma, and should have an indulgent sympathy with certain eminently human short-comings. In spite of his natural impatience of Boswell's lack of self-restraint and his vulgarity, and a certain weakness and egotism which made Mallory instinctively class him as a poor creature, yet he makes one realize that it was Boswell's overwhelming variety and, indeed, the very extent of his moral weakness which made him perceptive and sympathetic, and kindled in him the fire of impassioned idealism. Mallory's own feelings about the book are well expressed in a letter to Mr. Benson about the time it was finished. 'I have just returned from Wales full of life and good humour', he says. ' Before I went there I made a desperate effort and, at last, finished my book. I should like to impose it upon the public if it were possible. It seems to me a very curious hotch-potch from a literary point of view; I imagine that I have been learning to write while writing it and that it contains a series of experiments in expression: but I am fairly well satisfied with my account of Bozzy, so I think it had better appear if any one wants it, don't you?'

But while the book was still in its essay stage the time arrived when it became necessary for him to choose a profession. He had profited immensely by his education at Cambridge, although it had not been pursued on formal lines nor had he been particularly successful according to academic standards. But he had discovered that the world was teeming with interesting people, and interesting problems too, which each generation in turn had to solve to the best of their ability.

CHARTERHOUSE

Education of the best sort he had, but not the paper qualifications which pave the way to employment. He was devoted to Winchester, and a year or more before he left Cambridge his thoughts had turned toward the possibility of returning there as a master. He was at that time considering, too, but how seriously I do not know, the question of going into the church. His former housemaster in College at Winchester, Mr. M. J. Rendall, seems to have encouraged him in this. 'I have at last heard from Rendall', he wrote to Mr. Benson in 1907, 'who gives frank advice. He says that as I have nothing to teach and would probably teach it badly there is not the least chance of ever getting to Winchester. He thinks it would be a good plan to go to a private school for a year and then possibly to a good country parson as semi-pupil and semi-curate; after which he thinks I should want to go and work anywhere.

'I expect this is very good advice. I think it quite likely that I shall sometime become desperately keen on parish work of some kind; perhaps the only reason that I am not enthusiastic at present is that I'm at variance with so many parsons that I meet. They're excessively good, most of them, much better than I can ever hope to be, but their sense of goodness seems sometimes to displace their reason.

'The real reason for Rendall's advice, I gather, is that he feels I should make a bad schoolmaster and might make a good parson; and though he doesn't know me *very* well he feels it very strongly. In any case I'm glad he wrote candidly—I asked him to. . . . Your letter was most charming; but I have my doubts about the extent of my "moral influence"; and how far does it reach in the case of a schoolmaster?'

When the time came for him to leave the University he had given up the idea of the church but was still determined to be a schoolmaster, and in the autumn of 1909 he went to live in France with a view to perfecting his French.

In November he started for the Riviera, and took the opportunity, while on the way there, of making inquiries about the possibilities of some time at the Sorbonne. ' In Paris, where I stayed for some hours of Wednesday, I paid two important calls: M. Hovelaque the more eminent of the two men was also the more encouraging and seemed to think I might be lector at the Sorbonne, if I wished, next October. M. Legouis, who evidently took me for a schoolboy and didn't inquire my age, thought otherwise—so altogether there was not much to be got from them. I doubt if I should want the lectorship if I were able to get it; and the only other suggestion—of work in a French Lycée—does not at all appeal to me.'

He settled down for a while with a French family at Cabbé Roquebrune in the Alpes Maritimes. 'I like being here in spite of the distress it causes me to look at the hills and rocks so horribly unattainable.[1] I read, write, translate and even speak French with great energy. The conversations are apt to become mere fusillades since the sounds which I emit, being

[1] He had damaged his ankle by a fall while climbing the previous September and could not walk far.

both vehement and discontinuous, are rarely intelligible to any one but myself. The Bussys are pleasant people to live with, very cultivated and clever, but quite unaffected, simple, domestic, and sympathetic: I think I have made a good impression by kissing the little girl; it was she however who made the advances.'

He stayed about four months with the Bussys, during which he was able towards the end to explore the mountains which earlier had been so 'horribly unattainable'.

'It makes a great difference being able to walk further. My ankle is so far recovered that I have made the ascent of the highest hills—mountains I should rather call them for they are real mountain shapes with fine precipices and as high as Ben Nevis. They look better from below when one knows the summits. But Nature has limitations even here; it is an arid country. I miss the reposeful sight of green fields. To-day however there is a touch of spring in the air which makes me feel peculiarly happy: the few remaining birds, in a place where every one shoots and no game is too small, are making an effort to be cheerful. I don't expect to be here very much longer. I think of spending a month in Paris and returning to England early in April.' Before the month in Paris he managed to fit in a tour in Italy, as appears from another letter written before his return to England. 'My life has been somewhat nomadic for some time. Italy was glorious—Genoa, Pisa, Florence, I have really seen them at last, and their image is not effaced by the dingy impressions of the Quartier Latin. But I won't talk about Florence, it would be too like the pages of an art journal. I arrived here about a fortnight ago, after breaking the journey for a few days at Basel to see Hugh Wilson. He, poor creature! having spent two years in this enlightened country is now learning the German tongue; he is bearing it well, though a trifle hardened perhaps by the effort to produce those dreadful sounds in uncongenial company. But to return to the all-important ego: I was just beginning to feel, I must confess it, distinctly miserable, when a friend turned up, a Frenchman whom I knew in Cambridge, and bore me away to his charming home in the country. What a country it is! We were within motoring distance of Auxerre and to that enchanting old town I was taken one sunny day.

' The days in the country seem to have done me good—mentally I mean—for I now face Paris with a proud and cheerful heart. It is a curious life: a poky little room over a large street, lonely strolls in the Tuileries or the Jardin de Luxembourg which is nearby, and visits to the museums and other sights and sounds. I know very few people here at present; the man I see most of is a poet and literary critic and is very interesting on those subjects. He was a great friend of one Jean Morias who died just lately and is said to have been the greatest French poet of the XIXth century. Unfortunately my friend is blind. The term at the Sorbonne has just begun and I attended a lecture to-day. I expect I shall go to a good many, as there are interesting men there, and it improves one's French to hear it spoken in that

CHARTERHOUSE

kind of way. I hope to make some more acquaintances soon, through one or two introductions I have, but it is a slow business, and I hate meeting people with the feeling in the background that it is done as a duty on my part because it is useful to me to have Frenchmen to talk to! I expect to be here for a month, and after that I don't know. Perhaps I shall find myself in Cambridge, that is what I should enjoy most.'

Before the return to Cambridge he took a temporary post at the Royal Naval College, Dartmouth, which happened to offer itself immediately after his return to England. But this first experience in schoolmastering did not last long. ' This charming experiment is to end in a day or two. Lord! how pleasant it has been! I have even learnt to enjoy my " Early Schools "—five in a week! and out of bed at 6.15 punctually. I expect I have been a failure: it is almost impossible to be serious with youth. But it does every one good to be merry.

' The corpse of King Edward is to be interred to-day—perhaps you know. My feeling of gratitude to our late monarch is sadly dependent upon the fact that I have a whole holiday. I expect I shall spend it in wandering about the sad, cruel cliffs and looking at the blue-grey sea and the swirl of the waves.'

After this short time as a master at Dartmouth, Mallory was appointed an assistant master at Charterhouse. Here his absurdly youthful appearance became almost more than a joke. He was repeatedly mistaken by parents and others for one of his own pupils, and he used to say that the only compensation for looking so young was that it narrowed the gap between himself and boys in the school.

There is no doubt that he threw himself delightedly into the business of teaching and making friends at Charterhouse. He was full of ideas about the teaching of history and about the value of bringing humane letters to their proper place in education as its liveliest and most enduring part. But owing to his unconventional methods and his fiercely critical attitude towards the accepted public school routine, his activities were regarded with some disapproval by his elder colleagues. Since he himself valued education chiefly, perhaps, for its civilizing influence on the mind and character, he could not refrain from the attempt to conduct his educational activities in what he would have called a civilized way. He made considerable efforts to get into some sort of human contact with the boys, seeing what he could of them out of school hours, organizing expeditions with them to places of architectural or natural beauty, fostering their taste for literature and developing one for politics. The amount of energy and enterprise which he put into this side of his work was extraordinary, when one realizes how small was his natural aptitude for cultivating the acquaintance of the immature human creature. All the resources he possessed in literature and art were laid under contribution to his work. ' I've just begun Francis Place and am enchanted. I wonder if a cheap edition is coming out—it would be very good for my form. Such is the *arrière-pensée* of all my reading just now! By which token, do you know Jusserand's *Way-*

CHARTERHOUSE

faring Life in the XIVth Century? Having said what a good book it was for some time past, I have now taken the trouble to read it with a view to Chaucer in school—it's even better than I used to say.' He could not bring himself to treat great literature merely as a school subject, and used to exhaust his ingenuity in trying to find means to bring its worth and beauty into the cognizance of his pupils.

He was, as has been said, working perhaps too much outside the ordinary scholastic framework of a public school to be a very successful schoolmaster, but he must have been a rather exciting one. Friends visiting him at Charterhouse in the little house which he shared with one or two other masters, found the room a litter of books and papers —books in French and in English, modern plays which were being examined with a view to readings with his brighter spirits, Fabian tracts, reproductions or photographs of Greek sculpture or modern French paintings—all more or less drowned in a sea of essays from his form. He was a great believer in the essay and set them on the most divers and ingenious subjects, such as 'Candour', 'Popularity', 'Hypocrisy'. His friends, too, were called upon to furnish what they could—suggestions for essays, for books to be read, or even for original works of art. 'Duncan Grant', he writes, 'stayed with me last week-end and is to paint two pictures for my classroom!'

The other aspect of his work as a schoolmaster, and the doubtful success of it, was ever present to his mind: 'I am back, and *in media re* already. How *am* I to read *Paradise Lost* with a form of thirty boys ? I am perplexed day and night by considerations of that order.' It has always seemed to me that the fundamental problem of a school education, as it has to be carried out, is one of numbers. A limited experience of school teaching has left me with the conviction that the real problem only begins when the teacher has to deal with a collection of twenty or more intelligences of very varying calibre at one and the same time. For this purpose a certain technique has been developed—whether the subject be a language, mathematics, or science, it does not widely differ—which in the hands of a second-rate man may degenerate into the merest mechanical routine. In the hands of the average man of energy and resource it is a weapon of efficiency and value, even if it may not afford much opportunity for teaching of the highest order—for the hours remembered later as starting-points of intellectual growth. This technique of class teaching only the man of genius can afford to discard. If he is to do so he must be able to be humorous, strident, epigrammatic, suggestive, even poetical—to be able to seize and hold the attention of a class by the sheer force of his personality. Such a type of a man alone is able successfully to cast aside the traditional methods of his trade.

Mallory taught, I think, English, French, and History : all subjects which lent themselves to discursive teaching. His idea was that most boys started with the germs of an interest in learning and the arts, which must be developed by a sort of intellectual midwifery instead of being allowed to perish from lack of encouragement. He gave the impression that in the pursuit of this ideal he did not stick very closely to his subject but was inclined to talk at large. But such talk, to be really effective with a class, must be of the explosive and vital variety, whereas I always felt that Mallory had three drawbacks to his being, in this sense, a first-rate schoolmaster: his hurried and sometimes unintelligible utterance, his absence of pictorial imagination, and his lack of humorous initiative. He did not keep very good order, nor even attempt to, he said; and he used to relate with great satisfaction the tale of how the headmaster, passing his classroom door one day and hearing unaccustomed sounds from within, entered to find the class acting the part of the crowd in *Julius Caesar*, which they were then reading, with the greatest realism and enjoyment.

This was no doubt excellent, and may well have been the starting-point, for some, of a love of Shakespeare; but it is different when the part played by the class changes from active to passive. Boys will take a great deal of trouble to get away from their prescribed work; and if a master shows that he is capable of being drawn, and they learn how they can get him started on some disconnected topic, they will expend a good deal of ingenious diplomacy by expressing sufficient interest to keep the outflow going. But they do not listen very much or pay much real attention. It is enough that a friendly man is discoursing on general topics. The sound of a human voice is soothing, if you are not going subsequently to be examined on the matter discoursed of. You can think your own thoughts, even do your own work, if only you can keep him going. Such information, if vaguely uttered and without careful arrangement or design, shifting from topic to topic, is not very fruitful. Business-like boys hate it; original and able boys dislike being drenched with the substance of a single mind; dull boys wait under an umbrella of reserve until the shower is over. Perhaps a few boys may get a few ideas into their heads, and the fact remains that there were a good many ingenuous and enthusiastic individual boys, with whom he had made friends, who felt afterwards that they owed much in the direction of kindled enthusiasms to Mallory's talk and influence. Over all those with whom he established any personal relationship he would expend an infinity of interest and care. Feeling that they were his real friends in the place, he set himself to try to understand the difficulties of their years and to teach them to make things go right. As a result his instincts often led him to be on the side of the boys against established authority: a state of things which produced much internal conflict between his sympathy and his sense of responsibility, and accentuated the difficulties with his colleagues.

As a counterblast to the somewhat pronounced philistinism of the public school his influence must have been wholly desirable. It can seldom be other than good for a self-centred community with rigid and arbitrary conventions to be startled into shocked surprise by the irruption of an unfamiliar animal who ignores and even derides its cherished shibboleths. On more than one occasion Mallory was responsible for some flutter among the decorous upholders of public school proprieties: as when he and the poet Robert Graves (then a boy in the school) brought out a literary rival to the School Magazine. It was called the *Green Chartreuse*, and made its first (and probably only) appearance on Old Carthusian day, heralded by a poster of a more than life-sized monk in vivid green, quaffing with uplifted glass. The poster was executed by Duncan Grant in his most impressionist style and flaunted on the cricket pavilion throughout the match.

But I do not think Mallory felt, in the end, that his methods had been justified by results, and I remember his saying in later years that if he were to begin again with the same outlook and enthusiasm, but armed with his own experience, he would not attempt the same methods. The process was too exhausting and the results too nebulous. Even towards the close of his first year, ' Things go fairly well here ', he wrote, ' but it is very uphill work and there are a good many horrors when one sees people getting visibly worse through being at school. However, this last term has been very agreeable: several things got better: I got less irritable and found it easier to be severe without being angry. Also the other ushers seemed to be more friendly. There is only one common task I really dislike. Imagine me to-morrow morning teaching the smallest boys about the fall of man! what the devil is one to say? It was such a wholly admirable business and

God behaved so badly; mere petty jealousy! But there is a limit to the amount one may shock a person at one sitting.'

But this was in early days. He had gone to Charterhouse not much older in mind than he appeared in his face; with little or no teaching experience, and fresh from the society of lively young men of radical tendencies, arguing everything tenaciously and destructively; in the frame of mind when everything is an open question, and the hoarded wisdom and experience of the past is under suspicion of being mere pedantry and prejudice. He was at a stage when the world is seen chiefly in terms of literature, and when the disturbing adjustments needed for dealing with life as he found it stirred him to a contemptuous revolt. But even then he felt deeply about religion, and it was just this that made it so intolerable to have to deal with 'scripture' in a classroom. Soon after that time he gave up this part of his work entirely, and did not take it up again until after the war, when he had had time so far to straighten out for himself what he felt and thought, that he was able to teach something to boys which did not seem too far removed from the essentials of his own beliefs. As he gained in experience he became both happier and more effective, so that after two years at Charterhouse he could write in a much more buoyant vein than before: 'I'm enjoying life like anything. Some very interesting boys have come up into my Form, and it makes a lot of difference to have some leaven in the public school lump. I spent five days in Oxford lately, a very good time. Urquhart says that my destiny is to be a Don and pointed out that a number of History men are leaving Oxford. I think my job here suits me far too well for me to seek a change, even if I were wanted in Oxford, but there *are* moments when it seems a vital matter that I should have time to write.'

His engagement and marriage in 1914 at once completed one stage, so to speak, in his progress, and began another. The movement towards actuality, the transferring of his medium of expression from the sphere of literature to the sphere of real life, had been going on for a considerable time. His work at Charterhouse had had a good deal to do with this, forcing him to the practical necessity of dealing somehow or other, *himself*, with the fact of other people. It was no good merely to rub up his hair and quote Henry James over a form of boys, or his colleagues. There was no real escape—something more drastic was needed. He found himself compelled to bring to the task of dealing with all sorts and kinds of people something of the same care that he expended so willingly on his dealings with his friends. This was difficult for a person of his type. His impatience, his rapid preferences, his fastidiousness, his habitual preoccupation with impersonal topics were all in his way; and a continuous and protracted pegging away at any task which didn't command his enthusiasm was for him one of the hardest things in the world. To accomplish it at all he had to fall back, first on his real conscientiousness, and then on his own peculiar brand of half-humorous philosophy. This last always struck me as being an acquired characteristic in Mallory. He was not naturally philosophical by any means. His eagerness, his enthusiasm, his optimism were accompanied by their natural and corresponding opposites —a tendency to depression, impatience, and disgust at any failure. He liked to carry obstacles with a rush—the process of slowly overcoming them he did not ever enjoy. He did, however, frame his mind heroically to the task of dealing with his fellow-beings, and with a measure of success. And he became, as we have seen, a good deal happier in consequence. ' My life even now ', he wrote early in 1913, ' is one of the most pleasant I know. When the sun comes out again in this green paradise, I shall effervesce into a spirit. So you'd best come soon.'

By the end of 1913, however, Mallory seemed to have got as far as he could, for the moment, by himself, in the direction of reality—which is, whether he knows it or not, the goal of every man's search. He had made a resolute effort to tackle the problem of relationships, other than those of choice; he was already the most engaging, if the most elusive of friends; and the large realisms of mountaineering had left their mark upon him. But he could still be irresponsible if he chose—he was free to retire at any moment into the fastness of his impersonality; nothing had as yet happened to him to bring him under the common yoke of humanity, of intimate hopes, anxieties, loves, and fears. And his uncharted freedom had almost, one might say, begun to tire him.

CHARTERHOUSE

'Of course', he wrote at this time to a friend about to be married, 'I can only profess to believe that maidens and bachelors have the best of life: but I don't mind admitting to you privately that I consider them only half women and men.' At any rate, he was thoroughly ready for the adventure when it came. 'This will be a furious revolution to me, and all the better for that', he wrote of his engagement.

Mrs. Mallory's aunt, the late Mrs. W. A. Wills, wife of another great mountaineer, wrote to a friend: 'My niece, Ruth Turner, is engaged to be married. She is one of the "twice-born": a soul of the most crystal wisdom, simplicity and goodness—pure gold all through. She is going to marry a young Charterhouse master, George Mallory—I hope he is good enough for her, but it is hardly possible.'

The friend (who happened, unknown to Mrs. Wills, to be also a great friend of George Mallory's) had the exquisite satisfaction of writing back to say that her niece was marrying one of the rarest spirits of his generation, and that it sounded, on the whole, as though *she* might be nearly good enough for *him*!

Such was, indeed, the impression of both sets of friends—that here was a conjunction of two unique creatures. And the impression was not confined to their friends. A total stranger meeting both for the first time at some climbing centre, soon after their marriage, spoke of the shock of delight and astonishment which they produced. 'They seem too good to be true.'

'I must tell you some things about myself', Mallory wrote to Arthur Benson. 'It seems very difficult, but it ought not to be with you. The most wonderful thing about it is the knowing of someone else in a quite different way—I know what is noble in another human being much more deeply than ever before; the beauty of a soul known this way and the fineness and delicacy of it is overwhelming: and it really does make one good—already. But then, though it adds so much it changes nothing, only intensifies all that one thought best before. I'm more wholly devoted to my work here than ever I was; and Ruth shares my ideals, wants to know my friends among the boys, is prepared in fact to acquire the same devotion. I can't believe it can make life anything but more strenuous in the pursuit of virtue.

'When shall I see you again, I wonder, to talk about it? One has horrible qualms about friends after marriage—a feeling that it's more difficult to see them, though I doubt if it really is, and a haunting fear lest they should slide away.'

The 'furious revolution' began in earnest when the Mallorys settled down at Charterhouse early in 1915. George had hitherto lived a good deal in the clouds, or at least in a world of his own where literary and intellectual considerations were paramount. Practical concerns he had treated either with a casualness which bordered on the sublime or, if they seemed of sufficient importance, with a good deal of rather elaborate discussion. Now, in the house which they had made beautiful with such ardent and delighted care, he found himself surrounded to an unprecedented extent with what he called the apparatus of life—servants and furniture and social obligations. Moreover, to complete the revolution, his companion in this new life was a person of the wisest simplicity and a transcendent practicalness who dealt with all the everyday concerns of life with a prompt efficiency, and was wont to dispose of more weighty problems with summary and almost irreverent common sense. Seldom were two people more perfectly adapted to the purpose of modifying, rounding off, and completing each other. They had very much in common—notably courage, gaiety, generosity, and a love of all beautiful things. She was a craftswoman and could make beautiful things as well as appreciate them, and he could give expression to aspects of beauty of which she was perhaps only mutely aware.

Of the necessary adjustments to married life it was George, most probably, who had to make the larger share. His life had been very full before. Now his great impersonal objects of worship—mountains, art, and humanity in bulk, were confronted with a new personal devotion, and their place in relation to it had to be sought. It was soon found—more as an illumination shed on everything else by this new light than as a re-orientation of fixed objects. The gain to him was extraordinary: by one person finely known, he came to know all men better; by this profounder experience, this fresh security and happiness, he was at last brought into a more direct and personal contact with life at all points, no longer by a self-imposed effort, but by a spontaneous impulse.

Although Mrs. Mallory had hitherto done no climbing, she had in her the spirit of the mountaineer, only waiting to be aroused. She had always, she told me, been one of those who could never be at the foot of a hill without longing to be at the top. She had the physique, too, to be his companion upon all but the biggest expeditions.

They were married at the end of July 1914 and their honeymoon was to be his wife's introduction to the Alps. I had been climbing that year in Savoy during July and the plan was that we should foregather when they came out later. That plan the war demolished, but it did not prevent visits to North Wales and to the Lake District, during which Mrs. Mallory was taken up some of the most sensational of the rock-climbs to be found there. Previously to this the Mallorys had spent some part of their honeymoon in North Devon and Hampshire, walking and sleeping out. It must have needed a bad attack of Spy mania to disguise that radiant pair as suspicious characters, but arrested they were, one night when found in sleeping-bags on the shore near the New Forest.

Mrs. Mallory was destined never to climb with her husband in the Alps, but there were opportunities for short mountaineering holidays both before and after his joining the army, and she soon became a first-rate and devoted rock-climber. Her only experience of snow was during the Christmas holidays after their marriage, when we three spent a fortnight at the Pen-y-Gwryd hotel in North Wales. It was a most severe initiation: a time of gales and snowstorms, enough to daunt any but the stoutest hearted novice. I remember one occasion when we had climbed the 'Parson's Nose' and thought to go on over Crib-y-Ddysgil to the summit of Snowdon. On the ridge the gale was of hurricane strength, screaming and whirling the snow in all directions so that not a word was audible even when shouted in the ear. On our left was the snow slope down to Llyn Llydaw, and once over on that side there would be comparative shelter from the gale. But the slope in the driving snow and mist looked precipitously steep and terrifying. We were roped, Mallory in front, then his wife, myself last. When the wind at length became so fierce as to make breathing difficult and steady walking impossible Mallory decided that we must get down on to the sheltered side of the ridge. Explanations were impossible. I saw him point down the horribly steep looking slope and urge her in pantomime to take the plunge. From this, lacking our knowledge that it was in fact perfectly safe, she very naturally recoiled. And then there was enacted the most perfectly staged scene of mountaineering melodrama. Taking his wife by the shoulders, Mallory simply pushed her forcibly over the edge! I meanwhile, guessing what he was up to, stood down on the windward side to hold her rope. Next he jumped over also and soon we were all gasping in comparative peace while the wind still roared overhead. Mallory felt it was a great opportunity for instilling the necessary technique for the Alps, and I went on in front therefore so that he might have his pupil under his corrective eye. She was an apt learner, and even with his high standards he was full of commendation, although I do remember a sharp

'Damn you, dear, you mustn't do that' when she nearly pulled him out of his steps by a sudden jump forward.

I do not remember that we had a single day of comfortable climbing to encourage her; but in spite of the constant turmoil of rain and snow, and of the partial destruction of one of her boots by being left too close to the fire so that it had to be patched with a large piece of leather cut from a handbag, Mrs. Mallory was undaunted. I do not think she was ever so hardly tried again: the two other times which stand out in my memory are a week snatched in Skye in the August of 1918, and the last day of his climbing holiday in Wales, at Easter 1919, when we three, with Claude Elliott, made two new climbs on the Lliwedd face. The chief one, now known as the 'garter' traverse (because some two hundred feet or so below the 'girdle') gave Mallory the liveliest satisfaction. He had long felt that such a horizontal route across the face should be feasible and this last fine day had made it possible to work out the route before we left the hills.

All his friends must have their own memories of the Holt, the house at Godalming which was his home for the first seven years of married life. It stood perched on the edge of a steep combe, full of a tangled growth of scrubby oaks and hazels, in which, in spite of the houses all about, nightingales and black-caps nested and sang. From windows and garden, the eye travelled across the tree-tops to the playing-fields of Charterhouse, and beyond, down the valley of the Wey, to the hills behind Farnham;

while round to the south-west, the great bulk of Hindhead stood up against the sky; a real mountain shape, as Mallory used to say. It was not a beautiful house originally, nor ever externally, but technical skill in plenty was available to transform it for their use. A big bricked loggia was thrown out beyond the drawing-room, and continued in a broad low parapet wall overhanging the steep lower reaches of the garden—a perfect place to sit and swing the heels in discourse. For those who objected to sitting on brick, an oaken seat of vast and dignified proportions waited in the formal garden above the lawn, where two cemented lily-pools at once delighted the child and threatened the peace of the parent. Inside, the beauty of the house presented a surprising contrast to its rather unpromising exterior. Mallory had thrown himself into the work of beautification with great delight and more than his usual eagerness. His strong aesthetic sense had been able to express itself in a concrete way as never before, and he proved remarkably good at the art of producing the fact of beauty from the idea. The lion's share of the work fell to him, and he showed not only a discerning and adventurous taste in furniture and materials, but an extraordinarily sound judgement in the technical problems connected with the alterations. More than one of the schemes which he urged rather in opposition to his qualified advisers, proved, when carried out, to be exactly what was beautiful and right in its place. The inside of the house was a remarkable demonstration of the truth that artistic satisfaction need not call for unity of style. In that house were bright coloured stuffs of modern geometric design; fabrics and wall-papers from the Morris workshops; old oak, dark and solid; and new oak unstained and fresh from the workshop; all these heterogeneous units a sure eye for combinations had woven together, with the aid of carefully chosen rugs, into a pleasing and harmonious whole in which the eye no less than the body could rest satisfied. For their concern for externals worked upon a foundation of comfort, so that the boisterous irruption of small Mallorys always found grown-ups good tempered because soothed by one of the most perfectly restful drawing-rooms I have ever known.

The completed house was, as a house should be, a very perfect expression of them both. Perhaps the most individual place of all was George's study—a long low room on the first floor, with an abundance of books, an immense table presided over by a coloured stone group by Eric Gill, a cast of the ὕπνος, and one or two arm-chairs of a mellow and agreeable shabbiness. The black plumes of some Scots firs cut the sky at the level of the western window. Mallory loved this room and this window. He was exceptionally sensitive to his surroundings always; beauty and ugliness had a kind of spiritual importance for him, beyond their external significance; and the actual material perfection of this house of theirs really contributed to his peace and strength and capacity. I remember one small instance of this, among many. It was before one of his Everest lectures at Charterhouse. We had tea in the study. Mallory was nervous, clouded, and restless.

Presently, for some reason, he moved over to the window and his eye was caught by the waving tops of the firs against a windy western sky. 'Extraordinarily beautiful, that is,' he murmured, with a sort of relief breathing from him. Then he turned round with, 'It *is* a good house to live in—it's always doing something to help you like that.' His restlessness left him, and he was appeased and quiet for the remainder of the evening.

There need have been no anxiety about friends after marriage. Mrs. Mallory had been brought up in a house with almost medieval traditions of hospitality, and welcomed every one he brought, from the smallest boy to the most learned don, with the same simple and direct cordiality. She accepted sudden invasions with unruffled calm, seldom allowing the cares of the housewife to interfere with her pleasure in the guest. This was well, for George's ideas of entertaining were both expanded and optimistic. On Sundays and 'halves', the house swarmed with boys; the work of getting to know them was immensely simplified by having a spacious house of his own to invite them to. And friends and colleagues and neighbours were always being brought in, or, more frequently, coming of their own motion. It was such a good house to drop into! One of the two was always there, it seemed, and the other just coming; and there was generally some other friend whom it was delightful to meet, or meet again. There was always a welcome and a meal, and a sense of freedom and well-being for mind and body in that house—with any amount of good talk

—over the fire, or in the loggia, or strolling idly about the garden, perching on the low wall or on the great oak seat.

No picture of the Holt would be complete without mention of the Mallorys' near neighbours and constant visitors, Mr. Arthur Clutton-Brock and his family. Of all the friends of his later years there was no one from whom Mallory derived more, both of stimulus and of the spirit of toleration, than from Clutton-Brock. Many and long were the intimate evenings of talk between the two; and there can have been no one whose influence was more potent in the broadening and deepening of Mallory's character which became so evident in later years. It must always remain impossible to appraise, to weigh exactly, the gains that one person gets from another. But, intangible as they are, we do at least know that they are more important, enduring, and valuable than almost anything else in life. In the case of Mallory and his wife, no one, who knew George well before his marriage and after, could doubt that long and close contact with a person of qualities in many ways so different from his own, helped to steady, to round off, and to ease his character and his relations with other people in a very remarkable degree.

V
THE WAR

FOR a year or so after the beginning of the war Mallory was kept on at his work at Charterhouse. It was inevitable that the school and the boys should no longer have continued to fill his horizon as hitherto: his marriage alone would have made this impossible, but besides this, and the war, there were changes of circumstance which accentuated the break with the life he had been leading. The new house was not vacant until Christmas 1914, and even after that it was occupied by the workmen until well on into the spring, so that 'we lived cut off from Charterhouse by the river Wey; which generally made such big floods that I had a two-mile bicycle ride to get to school; it sounds a small matter but you know the kind of difference it would make in school life: I on one hill and the boys on another—there was a gulf fixed! And so I saw all too little of the boys. Nor was I completely happy to be living with my wife's people. They are very good people, but one doesn't want to live that way when one is married. To "settle down", that is what one wants; it sounds dull; in reality it's a sort of deliberate adventure. It's not that one wants to be a fixture in one of two easy chairs or perpetually to rub noses over the hearth, but rather to turn freely and curiously about with the chosen companion in chosen spheres until a new way of life is slowly evolved. It is evident that the life for two is very different from the life for one. It involves the battling of a constant shuttlecock—a battling spontaneously achieved for the most part, the expression of an amused energy, and a shuttlecock that seems to carry a variety of gay threads between the two until both are willing prisoners in a flexible parti-coloured web. I feel that our web-making has been sadly interrupted. When at last, only a fortnight or so before the end of term, we " came in " here, it was amidst many signs of incompletely organized conditions of civilized life. We have a very pretty view here and a warm bank; when I bask in the sun (as I don't expect to this gloomy day) I feel as happy as any one ought to feel. It is true, I'm afraid, that I've been too lucky; there's something indecent when so many friends have been enduring so many horrors in just going on at one's job quite happy and prosperous.

'I hear this morning that Rupert Brooke is dead of blood poisoning. I expect my friends to be killed in action, but not that way. It seems so wanton, and somehow it's a blow under the belt; he was a lovable person; and besides, he had gifts. I never much believed that he had it in him to be a great poet, but after all he might have become one.'

The sense of his own state of comparative comfort was constantly in Mallory's mind. It was, of course, heightened for him by the chance of his recent marriage and the great and increasing happiness that brought him. 'For my part', he wrote from Wales

THE WAR

during the first Christmas vacation, 'the war makes too little difference, so that I feel very uncomfortable about it. But it is a hateful background to one's thought, and an evil shadow over enjoyment. Happily the mountain air has blown away most of the clouds at present.'

Although to Mallory, as to all men, the war was an affair of overwhelming importance, it was not *the* great and heroic event of his lifetime as it was to many. During the first weeks, like every one else, he was much upset and excited and wanted to be off at once to France. While on his honeymoon—his marriage had been just a week before the declaration of war—he wired to his friend Geoffrey Young who was already with the armies in Belgium as a correspondent, to know if there were any way of being 'in it' without delay. And he refused to prolong the honeymoon among his favourite mountains of North Wales because he found it intolerable to be out of reach of news. But fundamentally his attitude towards the war was much more than a simple emotion of wishing to take part in a clash of arms where his friends were suffering and dying. With many people in England it was the war which first stirred them to think actively of international relationships and to consider the actions and characteristics of nations in their dealings with one another as being charged with moral values. It was otherwise with George Mallory. From the days when he read history at Cambridge he had always brought to the subject a liveliness of mind and a discursive freshness of interest in the present illustrations of historical fact which, though they would never have made a historian of him, might well have turned him, in other circumstances, into a politician. His strong moral preoccupation invaded this, like all other sides of his intellectual activity. The rightness or wrongness of national actions, and the motives from which they sprang, concerned him profoundly. It was also perhaps natural that his unusually conscious interest in human relationships on a small scale should have led him, in his historical thought, to a personalization of nationalities which made even his casual exposition of some international crisis a vivid and lively thing. Nations became to him like persons; their characters fair or ugly, lit by fine qualities or marred with weakness; their actions morally important. This personalization of nationalities can be overdone, but it was not, I think, by him; his was never the flimsy idealism of the sentimentalist which disregards the stubborn features of fact. It was simply that he could not tolerate the customary double standard of morals, one for persons and another for politics. He recognized, none the less, that political morality was a much later growth of the human mind, a much more complex, difficult, and refractory matter than personal morality, depending as it must upon a thousand considerations: considerations of economics, of diplomacy, of race, of trade, of the use of force and the possession of force, of social justice, and of national feeling.

The good life—for individuals, for all classes, for nations—and the comity of nations: these, with every year a deepening desire, were his ideal. It had always been his aim, when teaching history, to arouse in his boys an intelligent interest in foreign politics and in the sort of relationship which civilization ought to establish between nations no less than individuals. His ideal for education was a growth of the spirit, through freedom, into self-discipline, and the same process of evolution was what civilization should bring about between nations. More and more he turned to education as the only instrument with which to build up a civilization and to consolidate the ground gained by humanity. Education, more than anything else, could set man free from the worse part of himself; by education his imagination and sympathies were released from the narrow confines of personal interests, to see with the eyes of other races and to feel for other men. Education could confer that habit of sifting evidence, and of thinking hard and clearly, which alone makes a sane and unprejudiced judgement possible; it alone could focus feeling where feeling was right and proper—upon injustice, greed, or carelessness—and prevent it from trespassing in the province of clear thought, clouding facts and realities with its red or rosy mists.

Looking back at Mallory, as he stood among his contemporaries in the years from 1912 to 1920, it is extraordinary how well he seemed to exemplify his own theories. To meet him was always to receive a strong impression of being led to walk in a larger room where great and unfamiliar issues were present companions; to realize how thought was becoming his daily bread, and how much stronger and deeper his feeling was for being deaf to false catchwords and sham causes, and for concentrating on unwonted and less obvious aspects of affairs; and deeper than all was his feeling, afterwards to become a passion, that the good life could and must obtain, in international as well as in individual relations.

For a man holding these views, with these antecedents, the war at its first impact was the supreme disaster. It meant the break-down of a system, faulty it is true, and compromise-ridden, but which was still the fruit of centuries of human endeavour and represented, however poorly, the forces of order, justice, and civilization. It was a catastrophic interruption of human progress; a hideous resurgence of uncivilized and antisocial forces; the destruction for the time being of the good life as he knew it; and the grave of a thousand hopes. War in itself seemed to him so intolerably wrong that almost nothing could excuse it. It was a ghastly evil that sane men must bear as best they could. It was natural that for him there should be no joyful leap to meet the occasion, but what looked like a rather horror-stricken detachment.

As an escape from despair his sanguine spirit seized upon some of the earlier events as heralding the advent of a new era in international relations, when militarism and the forceful suppression of small nations should disappear, and with them the root causes for the perpetuation of strife. 'I feel', he wrote during the first weeks, ' almost as if a tide of centuries has swept over us in the last fortnight, we are basking in the sun and watching the dawn of tremendous hopes. The Czar's proclamation to

THE WAR

Poland has knocked the wind out of me, and if only it wasn't for those blessed Balkan States and that rotten Turkey I should be full of hope of seeing the Golden Age. In any case it seems that Europe is to take another great leap along the good path she began to tread in 1789. Prussian militarism must vanish now; and I believe in the German civilization if only it is given a fair chance of development; their music could only come from the party of the angels. And a free united Poland is, or may be, the biggest possibility for Good that ever we've dreamed of. I suppose I'm very sanguine, but after all Europe has made leaps before; 1830 was a very big leap; so I shall hope for another.'

When able no longer to buoy himself up with hopes of this kind he became appalled by the war as a vast tidal wave of unreason, in which all regard for truth and beauty was drowning, swamped by the emotional and propagandist flood. There was no one more determined on the necessity of winning in the fight, but he feared lest, in the process, we as a nation should lose all sense of the responsibility of victors. Even about the war, people must be made to think, free from passion or confusion. The horrors of the Press, even after he was in France, were hardly less real to him, and infinitely more corrupting, than the horrors of the field, for they signified the submersion of all spiritual, beneath material, aims. 'I feel that our Kultur is brought to the test along with the rest; it can show its worth very well by the attempt still to see clearly and judge without prejudice. The point of application pricking me most keenly at the moment prompts the action of a Felton or Ravaillac; and the modern victims you have already agreed should be the lords of the Press. Can we endure it any longer? I should be sorry actually to stick the dagger if another remedy could be found. But what is to be done? The vilest is that such things only are because they pay. What an indictment of a nation!

' I've been thinking much lately about possible conditions of peace. It's all so much more difficult now we're learning the worst about Germany; our reserve of patience seems to have gone; I'm afraid no one's going to resist cries of revenge, let alone listen to cries of mercy—and I don't know that I want them too. The more we know, the more deeply what we began by calling Prussianism seems to pervade all Germany. In spite of all this I am wondering whether it wouldn't be possible to form some society for combatting, when the moment arrives, the nonsense which is sure to appear in the Press about terms of peace, &c., and instilling some sensible notions; it would have to be done by a very widely organized series of public lectures; if a sufficient number were delivered at the right time they might have a considerable result. What do you think? There would be plenty of folk willing to do it and able to agree, I should think, in an aversion to the old Grab-Policy which has prevailed in the past.

' My idea is not to discuss terms of peace publicly at this time, only to make ready to do so when the moment arrives. Of course, any talk now must be hypothetical. But we can arrive at principles now, and ultimately demand that whatever arrangements are made agree with them. I mean, for instance, we can decide whatever happens that we don't want the grab-system applied at all and we don't want any plums for ourselves at the end of the war. I am far from imagining that England will necessarily be able to get things done as she wants: but it is none the less important that she should demand the right things. And, considering the influence the Press has and what it is like, I should be sorry if no attempt were made to form opinion by other means. The sort of thing I foresee, if we crush Germany, is Northcliffe clamouring for the Kiel Canal, the *Morning Post* agitating on the lines of the anti-German League, and the radical Press shouting for a republic Germany.... Meanwhile we must set our teeth.'

Enough has probably been said to explain why much would be needed to make Mallory feel that he would be doing better work as a soldier than as a schoolmaster, even if the action of the Charterhouse authorities, in saying definitely that he could not be spared, had not settled the question for him during the early stages. But as the war dragged on the compulsion to take a more active part came upon him. He felt at last with all his being that the good life had its deadliest foes in the Central Powers, and that for the moment the blows struck in its cause must be struck with shells and bayonets. That once settled, his way was again clear, and his realism and his sense of facts made him see the war more plainly in terms of 'killing Germans' than many who had joined earlier and with a readier enthusiasm.

As one who at school had started life, so to speak, as a Woolwich candidate, it was appropriate that Mallory should have joined the artillery. Ignorant of this early bent, and knowing him only as an enthusiast for history, literature, and the arts, any one must have been astonished at the ease with which he took to the details of range-finding and at his delighted interest in the mysteries of the slide-rule. Behind his love of words and literary form, there lay a real respect for the exactitude of mathematics and a hatred of all muddle and inefficiency.

After the usual delays of training he joined the Expeditionary Force early in May 1916. 'I have just been ordered to France', he wrote on the 3rd, 'and cross to-morrow night. I can't pretend to be bursting with joy at this moment; the personal tie is too overpowering, but I believe I'm completely happy in the insidest part of me and the thinking part. So far I've been a mere schoolboy in khaki, so you may imagine I'm feeling, with my inferior knowledge and utter inexperience, one of the humblest of God's creatures and not over-confident; although its a triumph too that one has become a soldier, so far as appearances go, in so short a time; and naturally I'm very happy to be that.'

He was posted to the 40th Siege battery and for some months led the ordinary life of a subaltern 'scurrying round to establish communications, to collect information from the infantry, and to select points of advantage for observation posts. . . . Really these expeditions aren't so bad; the point is, I suppose, that they *are* of an adventurous nature and that one has companions. It is curious how often I am taken back to the Alps—partly through an association in the code of conduct, and partly I think because of their wonderful *cleanness*. We're now living in old trenches, indescribably filthy. Happily I have a hole dug in clean earth (its astonishing how one grows in love of Mother Earth; I could stroke this clay with affectionate hand); here I can retire in high solitude and fix my mind in praise of BED. It's there I'm sitting and its the temple of thought. You can imagine how one may feel about it after several fervid days spent in the front line. I had a shocking experience some days ago—two of my signallers killed outright; they were walking a little way behind me carrying a reel of wire and were caught by shrapnel before they had time to dodge into the communication trench; such good fellows too. I've had three other casualties in a short time from my small parties.'

This was written in August 1916, to Mr. Benson. A month later he wrote to the same correspondent and in the same reflective mood. 'I wish I knew more about George Gissing; I am reading *Born in Exile* at present and am greatly impressed by it. He really goes into the psychology of what he calls " Militant egoism ", and how important that is! I'm sure that a great many young men experience something of this; it was very common at Cambridge when I was up, and my own share is no secret between you and me. I wish I had read this book in

GEORGE LEIGH-MALLORY

those days; I might have come quicker to a lot of things I've learnt since.

'It is necessary to sort me out, when you think of the horrors of war, as only participating in a mild degree. For me it is like some ill-devised and frozen picnic when every one has determined not to enjoy himself. However, I do get some fun out of it; although I believe the worst about the war is that it is such a poor subject for humour. It is hard to laugh expansively even at the most laughable sayings of the Kaiser, the results of the state of mind he reflects are too terrible and we can't detach ourselves; although I suppose there are people who laugh exultantly at the folly of a foe. The sublime humour of the trenches, I'm inclined to believe, is made behind the lines—very likely by the infantry themselves when they go back; at all events I've seen nothing of it; men look serious enough under shell fire and speak very little. Of course I don't mean that there aren't things and people to laugh at in any way of life. I heard yesterday of a very self assured little Scot who was on our course at Weymouth; he was so much frightened during the performance of his duty at the latrine by the whistle of an Archie shell case that he attempted the most precipitate of flights into a shell hole, his trousers down gyved to his ankles; and his fall was so violent that he has been invalided home with a hurt leg. One requires to know the bombast of the man to appreciate this career.

'It's not true, in my case, that one doesn't mind the horrors of war. But in self-defence they must not be allowed to affect the nerves; I have ceased to have any feeling about corpses unless they disgust my nose; on the other hand it always pains me to see a wounded man. The horrors are no longer horrible but tragedy remains pitiable. I still regret my two signallers; it was a tragic end to hours of good fellowship. But then again I am not depressed by what pains me; I suppose, if we agree that men get used to painful scenes (and women even more easily I expect) it is meant that the mind comes to appreciate them very quickly. One looks and is pained and goes on his way; an image has passed into the consciousness and can be recalled as easily as one that was absorbed more slowly; but it will not be recalled again and again; the mind knows all about that, and the value of it, and however ready the fount of pity may be one refuses to tap it reiteratively for the same cause.

'From which you will gather that I keep in good spirits. I had quite a thrill in the trenches yesterday on seeing a really beautiful face. What a subject for a poem (which will never be written)! Generally speaking most of the officers to be seen there either have an air of intending to fight, an assertive pugnacity, or, what is more unpleasant to see, they obviously hate the whole business—more pitiful, at all events. This R.F.A. man was sitting quietly beside his signaller waiting on events; he had a rare dignity; for him clearly there were things beyond his surroundings; he had beautiful visionary eyes which looked at me thoughtfully before he answered my remarks, and I felt that had I timidly asked him

"Do you hate it all very much?" he would probably have replied with infinite reserve, "Why yes, sometimes I hate cheese without bread, tea without milk, and meat without potatoes."'

Early in 1917 the fact that Mallory could speak French with some fluency led to his being attached as liaison officer with the French artillery, and he visited a number of anti-aircraft and other batteries. In a letter written about the middle of February 'I have been very happy with these people', he says, 'they are very agreeable and intelligent. *Serieux* I suppose the French would call them, and I like that. This business has been a success from the personal point of view and not much use otherwise. I sent in a report after seeing the Aviation; I was quite pleased with it—considering I only had twenty minutes there and it was necessary to see a great deal and at the same time absorb all the details of a complicated organization. The General and Colonel both rang me up to thank me for it—the latter saying that it was going on to the Corps and I should "probably get a D.S.O. or something!" which I take to have been a manner of speech. I've really taken a lot of trouble here to find out about French Artillery; I know far more about it now from a general point of view than about our own. To understand an organization so nicely adjusted as theirs gives me a very considerable pleasure.

'Since coming to France I have regarded inefficiency in my own person as the unforgivable sin —I have actually on one or two occasions experienced a sense of sin almost new to me in its intensity.

THE WAR

To-day I have experienced a feeling hardly less intense with regard to others. For this Army of France, suffering, experimenting, learning, organizing, the war has been one long continuous effort of will, and intellect. Now it is braced to a state of fine efficiency beyond what the British Staff has been able to imagine; and it is bursting with hope like a chestnut bud in April. Patient accuracy, clear thought, science;—everything has been built on these; and above all on the " Système D ". And yet in this army I met to-day a corner of dingy muddle showing no more intelligence than one might expect to find in the office of a provincial solicitor. This is apropos of some French artillerymen who clearly were unequal to their job through sheer idleness. (The " Système D " means—in two words—" Ingenious improvization ", or " Initiative in overcoming difficulties ").'

It is hard to say of any one what the actual experience of modern warfare meant to him. Some part may be expressed, more perhaps becomes apparent in later life, but most is of the order of a secret, scarcely perceptible, modification, hard to realize, and harder, if not impossible, to describe. Certain effects the war undoubtedly produced in Mallory. He was obliged to live for long periods at a time in close daily contact with all sorts of people whose mode of life and thought differed as widely as possible from his own and he certainly gained in sympathy and tolerance by this, although not without a struggle. ' I'm sure there never was such a lover of his own company as I am. I hope I have learnt how to suffer an excess of companions in a confined space, but I can never forgive or forget the excess of time that passes away with no addition to one's store of amusing thoughts.' One gains from his correspondence a strong sense of his carrying on a life apart, a life of conscious thought and self-examination, through all the monotony of his months of training and through the disorder and ugliness of his time in France. His letters are full of the books he has read and got pleasure from—' but of what use telling you what I've read ', he breaks off, ' since we can't talk about it '—full, too, of attempts to probe beneath the surface of things and to see clearly the problem of ultimate values which the precariousness of all men's lives made more pressing than ever. ' I was wishing the other day ', he wrote in 1916 just before going out, ' that I could know the individual minimum, as I call it to myself, for every one—the least a man would be content to leave behind as his share of life accomplished. Wouldn't one know something if one could know that? '

He always felt passionately the need for keeping alive the life of thought, both as a personal and a national thing, and it was characteristic of his attitude towards the war that part of his time while in training to go abroad was spent in writing a pamphlet addressed to the boys and girls of England [1] upon what they could do, while still at school, for their country. It is an appeal to the youth of England to spend their years of enforced education in fitting

[1] *War Work for Boys and Girls.* Allen & Unwin.

themselves, by reading and by *thought*, to form a just, wise, and well-informed public opinion, and its chief aim is to show ' how the nation's good is deeply involved in this matter of national thinking ' (ibid., p. 5). It is an admirable statement, for its size, of the importance of public opinion in national affairs, of more than ephemeral value, and deserves a wider circulation than it has ever had. ' We must think ', he concludes, ' with all our minds; . . . think with imagination and sympathetically; think passionately and, not less, think calmly, without prejudice and critically—think, and when we think, devote ourselves to learning what is right for England.'

Mallory's feelings about personal inefficiency expressed in a letter from France already quoted, were certainly much intensified by the war, and in this respect it left a permanent mark upon him. People who only knew him well during and after the war have found it hard to credit stories of his early haphazard methods in dealing with everyday affairs, so thoroughly was the lesson learnt. As usual, he probed below the surface to discover wherein the elements of real efficiency consisted. During his period as liaison officer he had an opportunity of seeing our own war machine through foreign eyes, an experience which he valued greatly. One story told him by the Frenchmen seemed to bear upon this question of efficiency: with half-amused and half-scandalized bewilderment they related how, when an English brigade had taken over some French trenches on the Somme, the young subalterns were to be seen walking coolly about above the trenches whose whereabouts the previous occupants had carefully concealed. 'Ces Messieurs anglais sont fantasTIQUES!' was the comment. Fantastic courage was all very well, but routine efficiency still required intelligence and self-restraint to reap its full harvest; and behaviour which could destroy in a careless moment the work of months had no place in it.

This respect for a quiet practical efficiency, and a redoubled intolerance of laziness in the sphere of ideas, were perhaps, for Mallory, the final lessons of the war. It had certainly deepened in him a sense of the importance of ideas. Amidst a welter of physical destruction ideas, at least, could and *must* survive. The good life, for men and nations, depended upon right ideas being thought out clearly and held with a passionate conviction by the largest possible number of people; they must be held with a conviction and formed with a clearness which no political jugglery or unscrupulous journalism could betray or confuse.

VI

EVEREST

THE RECONNAISSANCE AND ASSAULT

As soon as he was demobilized, in the spring of 1919, Mallory returned to Charterhouse. The shape of Everest had not, at that time, appeared upon his horizon, but the lines along which he had been developing were such as to make him ready for the adventure when the question was first mooted. The dissatisfaction which he had always felt at many of the effects of a public school education were only deepened by the war and by his wider experience, not of boys in training but of the made man. Proud as the public schools might well be of the part they had played as the nurseries of a national tradition of leadership and ready sacrifice, were they conscious also of the other ideal, of fitting men to be intelligently happy and reasonably good? That was the problem of education which was of primary importance to Mallory, and he expressed his misgivings in a form which is worth quoting. ' I have imagined myself', he wrote, ' to be confronted by the accusing finger of a father. "I gave you a boy", he seems to say, "with the unspoilt beauties of boyish qualities. He wasn't exquisitely refined, nor was he a paragon of virtue, nor yet supremely talented. He was a decent little chap, truthful, honest, and persevering. He had a gay roguish way of fun, and his laughter was without malice or contempt. I hardly ever knew him short of a job. He was a creature of the open air, with an interest quick to be aroused. Books were not a great interest with him; but he knew how to consult them for information about birds or flowers, or whatever he was pursuing. In all a pleasant companion full of young curiosity, a healthy animal, a proper English boy. And to me how much more than that! For he had an open heart; open to me at least, and to his mother, so that we could easily know him " ... " And what has school done for my boy? " he goes on to inquire. " It is a different tale I have to tell now. My son is a capable athlete; he can take hard knocks and give them; he won't funk and he knows it; he has any amount of what he would call ' guts '. I'm glad of that. And he has something that might pass at a pinch for manners —a method of light conversation, an assurance, an address. But of manners in the finer sense, the manners that ' makyth man ', he knows little enough. He may offer a glass of lemonade to a lady, and at best he may do it gracefully. But you are not to imagine that he puts others before self; he has never a serious thought about their feelings or their interests. He has no desire to look below the surface of men's minds, no delicacy of approach, no more than a scant degree of modesty. Superficial and self-satisfied, he is disastrously ill equipped for making the best of life. I cannot discover that he has acquired from any honest thinking the right to a single opinion: and yet he is more than sufficiently opinionated and easily contemptuous of any opposite view.

THE RECONNAISSANCE AND ASSAULT

He is no less mentally a coward than he is physically courageous, and as prejudiced as he is dependent. I find his whole scale of values petty and unenlightened; he judges by little forms and conventions without seeing to the heart of things; he will notice a man's tie and his socks without remarking that he is a liar; he will prefer him for being rich; and he will dub him eccentric if he is particularly in earnest. For literature, music, art, he cares nothing, and for Nature little more. He seems to have no interest beyond cricket and a motor bicycle, and no taste beyond the music hall vulgarities. It would be difficult to find any one more readily bored. Nice things to say about one's own son! But I have tried to be just. Put him, you may say, in a responsible post and see how he will acquit himself. It would not perhaps be an ignoble performance; and that's so much to the good. But are you to take the credit? We can most of us rub along without making a mess of things; like others, I expect he will be able to muddle through; you haven't destroyed that capacity. But his education was to give him so much more. Perhaps I am partly to blame. But from the first I was helpless. When I gave him to you, he was lost to me. I knew him no longer and couldn't know him. The open flower closed and its beauty was hid. In vain I attempted to follow him into the new and strange world. His lips indeed spoke but his heart was closed from me and from his mother. We gave you youth with the bloom of childhood—you have rendered, not indeed Man, but youth again with Man's hard skin."'

There must be many parents who would echo the

general tenor of this indictment, although one may doubt the fairness of laying the blame for the most part with the school. The fundamental educational failure, as Mallory saw it, in the present system is the lack of continuity; the sharp division into alternating periods, remote and unrelated in the occupations which filled them, no less than in manners and atmosphere. Which of us, looking back, must not admit that we were totally different beings when at home and at school? And in weight of influence the school, during those years, has an overwhelming advantage, both from the length of terms and from the greater vividness and constant novelty of impressions.

When Mallory returned from the war he was not tired of teaching, but he was tired of his part in the educational machine; tired of imparting elementary knowledge, and tired of the sort of intellectual bribing and caressing which he had found necessary to stimulate the interest of boys. He was reaching out after other surroundings, in which he would be unhampered by what he felt as a cramping tradition. His first idea was for the founding of a new school. The plans for this were discussed at great length and drawn up in considerable detail. Since he felt that the greatest source of weakness among boarding schools was that the best enthusiasms of home too often find no encouragement there, and vice versa, he placed in the forefront of his plans for the new school the condition that the parents should undertake actively to co-operate in the efforts of the school. This co-operation was not to be attempted by any

THE RECONNAISSANCE AND ASSAULT

large demonstration, such as a conference of parents, but by a continuous effort on both sides to keep in touch, and so make term and holidays complementary influences in a continuous process of education. The co-operation from both sides was to call for an effort of sympathy which would go beyond generalities and be greedy of details. Reports from the school would be written not only with the idea of telling how a boy was getting on, but also of a more general nature, giving brief accounts of any particularly interesting courses of lessons, showing whither they lead and what ideas a pupil may have been expected to imbibe. They would describe also any school enterprise involving the communal activity of the pupils, such as farming: for the life of the school was to be grafted on to an estate with at least one farm of a general character, so that games might be made to alternate with agricultural work, and to give place to it entirely at certain seasons, when the children would be made to feel that every active hand was needed for productive work.

While these plans for the school were being thought out Mallory was carrying on his work at Charterhouse, besides a variety of other activities. In 1919 he revisited the Alps after a separation of seven years. In 1920 he went again, and at the end of the same year his passionate interest in the Irish question led him to go and investigate for himself the conditions in that stricken country. One can imagine how the expedition appealed to his love of adventure. On foot, with a rucksack and without credentials, he walked from place to place through all that part where killing and burning were a commonplace of every village. This Irish adventure is important, not so much for its own sake, but as indicative of the restless energy and, too, the dissatisfaction with his job as a schoolmaster which was driving him to cast about for new fields of activity. How easy to sit at home and say that one really ought to go to Ireland and investigate the truth for oneself! And how few of us would pack up our things and go!

His return to the Alps the year before had affected him profoundly. 'The Alps were incredible', he wrote. 'I hadn't realized how little one could keep them in his head. It was more thrilling than I can say to see them again—even from the train as we came up the valley to Chamonix, and much more at close quarters. We had three first-rate expeditions besides two most interesting ones from an instructive point of view, a failure on the Requin and a highly successful short cut to the Col du Géant by the wrong side of the Glacier, where we explored some of the finest crevasses I have ever seen. Our other climbs included a new route on the now famous Grepon-Charmoz face above the glacier de Trelaporte, up to the arête of the Charmoz which one sees from Montanvert, above the Aiguille de la République. For sustained endeavour and dramatic moments the climb far excelled any rock climb I know and, I suspect, all but very few that I don't know. We seemed completely cut off, about 3.30, by the vertical wall of a great tower, when only 100 feet below our arête, and from that point obtained our

THE RECONNAISSANCE AND ASSAULT

first clear view of a formidable vertical step in the arête further on . . . a traverse under an overhang and a hair-raising performance up a very steep wall solved the first difficulty, and we reached the main crest very thankfully at 4.15 p.m. The Aiguille du Midi was in a way our finest expedition, with glorious snow and ice work—a new route, too, I believe. . . . I got very fit and was really very pleased to find myself less incompetent than I expected, more particularly on ice and snow.'

I have quoted this letter at some length because, with the exception of the bad weather season of 1912, when he and Hugh Pope and Harold Porter carried out almost the only notable climb of the year, a new route up the Dent Blanche, this return to the Alps after seven years was the first occasion on which Mallory may be said to have reached the position of the fully equipped mountaineer, planning and executing expeditions without guides and with the co-operation only of his own contemporaries. In the following year he was again leading a guideless party, of which I was one, and I remember being repeatedly impressed by his genius for picking out a complicated route, both from a distance, and in detail when it came to close quarters.

Almost immediately on his return from Ireland he was invited to join the first Everest expedition. 'I am faced with a problem', he wrote to me, 'which throws all others into the background—Everest?' Coming at this moment, while he was already contemplating a move from Charterhouse and when, as a climber, he must have felt himself at the top of his powers, it was inevitable that this call to new fields of adventure and to the most supreme mountaineering enterprise should have been irresistible. 'I hope it won't appear to you a merely fantastic performance', he wrote to his sister. 'I was inclined to regard it as such when the idea was first mooted a few weeks ago, but it has come to appear now, with the help of Ruth's enthusiasm, rather as the opportunity of a lifetime. . . . The future bears rather an adventurous aspect altogether; I have resigned my mastership at Charterhouse, as I intended to do in any case after the summer. I shall be starting for Tibet early in April and have no very definite idea what I shall do after I come back in the autumn—except that there's much in my head which is asking to be written.' 'I am just fixed for Everest', he wrote on February 10th, 1921, to his old climbing companion, Geoffrey Young. 'I lunched with Farrar yesterday to meet Raeburn and Younghusband, and the old boy made me a formal offer which I accepted. It seems rather a momentous step altogether, with a new job to find when I come back, but it will not be a bad thing to give up the settled ease of this present life. Frankly I want a more eminent platform than the one in my classroom—at least in the sense of appealing to minds more capable of response, I expect I shall have no cause to regret your persuasions in the cause of Everest; at present I'm highly elated at the prospect and so is Ruth: thank you for that. My view about the party is chiefly that it is inadequate in numbers— there is no margin. Raeburn says he doesn't expect

THE RECONNAISSANCE AND ASSAULT

to get higher than about 25,000 feet; Dr. Kellas presumably will get no further; so that the final part is left to Finch and me, and the outside chance that Wheeler or Morshead will take to climbing and make a success of it. Perhaps after all I shall be the weakest of the lot; but at present I feel more doubtful about Finch's health.'

Mallory's misgivings about Captain Finch's health and about the other two members of the climbing party were unfortunately well founded. At the last moment the former's place had to be taken by Mr. Bullock, a climber of fine physique but very limited experience; Mr. Raeburn's health broke down so that he took no part in the climbing; and the tragic death of Dr. Kellas during the journey through Tibet, before ever he had set eyes upon Everest at close quarters, cast a gloom over the whole expedition. It was an event which Mallory felt very deeply, for he had taken an instant and strong liking for this strange man upon the moment of their first meeting at Darjeeling. Born and trained as a chemist in Aberdeen, Dr. Kellas had formerly been lecturer in Chemistry at the Middlesex Hospital, but had devoted the last ten years of his life almost wholly to a study of the physiological effects of climbing at high altitudes. All his life he was a devoted mountaineer, first in Scotland, then in the Alps, and lastly among the Himalaya. All his expeditions were made by himself with his coolies, and of many of the journeys there is little or no record, but it is known that in the one season of 1910 he made no less than ten new ascents to above 20,000 feet; and that his final achievement was to reach 23,600 feet on Kamet, in Garheval, in 1920. The manner of his joining the expedition has been described by Mallory in a letter to his wife and is worth quoting for the lively picture it gives of this uncouth and attractive figure.

During the days of rest before the start from Darjeeling the party were being entertained at Government House. ' On our first night the governor gave a swagger dinner-party for the expedition. It was a wonderful show. We assembled about twenty-five couples according to a printed list, of which a copy had been supplied to every one, and in the drawing-room we were very adroitly manœuvred by the two A.D.C.'s. His Excellency entered and amid complete silence made the circuit of the room and shook hands with every one. In the drawing-room a host of native servants, wearing long red coats ornamented with gold and silver braid, pushed our chairs in as we sat down and poured champagne into our glasses after every sip or so it seemed. Music played all the time, but not so loudly as to make conversation difficult. We all rose during dessert, following H.E., who behaved like clockwork and proposed the health of the King-Emperor; we were silent while the band played some bars of God save the King, and I observed that most people's eyes were where they ought to be—fixed in a steady stare across the table . . . and so on. Everything went with a click.

' I love Kellas already. He is beyond description Scotch and uncouth in his speech—altogether uncouth. At the great dinner-party he arrived ten minutes after we had sat down, and very dishevelled, having walked in from Grom, a little place four miles away. His appearance would have formed a good model for the stage for a farcical representation of an alchemist: he is very slight in build, short, thin, stooping, and narrow-chested; his head a very curious shape, and made grotesque by veritable giglamps of spectacles and a long, pointed moustache. He is an absolutely devoted and disinterested person.'

Of Kellas's death Mallory wrote very fully to Geoffrey Young and to myself: ' He had spent some two months climbing under very severe conditions, and ill-nourished, and he got back to Darjeeling only about a week before we started. He travelled to Phari with the second party and arrived there suffering from enteritis, and had a day's rest there. He was very anxious to come on and the alternatives were unsatisfactory: he could only have gone back two stages to Yatung, where there is no medical officer, but a good bungalow and a comparatively mild climate at 9,000 feet. He was taken on in the expectation that he would be better in a day or two, and if not sufficiently strong by the time we reached Kampa Dzong could be much more easily sent down from there into Sikkim. Some form of litter was arranged and he was carried on each day with his own head coolie-bearer looking after him. The most tragic and distressing fact about his death is that no one of us was with him. Can you imagine anything less like a mountaineering party? It was an arrangement which made me very unhappy, and which appalls me now in the light of what has happened.

And yet it was a difficult position. The old gentleman (such he seemed) was obliged to retire a number of times *en route* and could not bear to be seen in this distress, and so insisted that every one should be in front of him. We grew accustomed to leaving him behind to some extent after the first part of a day's march, and expended our *petits soins* in seeing that everything was ready for his arrival, or going out to meet him and walking in the last mile or so. After all, there was nothing one could do for him if one did stay to see him, and he didn't want it. We were assured that he was getting along all right about half way on the last day, and it was a great shock when a coolie came on after we had all reached Kampa Dzong and said that he had died. Wollaston, of course, was completely taken by surprise.

' This is a very dull, impersonal way of writing. You will perceive the object. Wollaston is more my friend than any one in the party and has been greatly distressed. I am afraid some folk at home may be inclined to criticize him, and this you may be able to prevent.

'It was an extraordinarily affecting little ceremony, burying Kellas on a stony hillside: a place on the edge of a great plain looking across it to the three great snow peaks of his conquest. I shan't easily forget the four boys, his own trained mountain-men, children of nature seated in wonder on a great stone near the grave, while Bury read out the passages from the Corinthians.'

From this point, Kampa Dzong, the reconnaissance of the mountain may be said to have begun.

THE RECONNAISSANCE AND ASSAULT

'We are just about to walk off the map—the survey made for the Llasa expedition. We've had one good distant view of Everest, and I'm no believer in the easy North face. It's beginning to be exciting.'

The story of this reconnaissance has inevitably been thrown into the background by the more dramatic and highly organized efforts of two subsequent expeditions. But what an astonishing achievement it was! The tragic death of Dr. Kellas on the day before their first glimpse of Everest had robbed the climbing party, not only of all Himalayan experience but of any one with a knowledge of the language. When the little climbing party started from Tingri Dzong on June 23rd, it consisted of the two Englishmen, sixteen coolies, a sirdar, and a cook. It had been assumed by both Mallory and Bullock that their experienced leaders would be at hand to give necessary orders for organization in any dialect that might be required; whereas they now found their only means of communication with the sirdar to be about 150 words which Mallory had written down in a note-book.

For the next month they were dependent for all their climbing, which reached 23,000 feet, upon such organization as could be built up from this small company in spite, rather than with the help of, the sirdar, who proved himself 'a whey-faced treacherous knave, whose sly and calculated villainy too often, before it was discovered, deprived our coolies of their food.' They were not long in experiencing the sort of trials which must have called for an infinity of patience and self-reliance in that utter remoteness, and when cut off from any base. A few miles out from Tingri the four pack animals they had hired were perceived to be heading in the wrong direction. By no means certain of the right one (Everest of course had not then been located from near at hand), they were trusting to the guidance of local drivers, but the line these were taking was an impossible one. An interminable three-cornered argument followed. It appeared that the guides intended to take five days to a village which previous inquiry had led them to believe should be reached in two. And it *was* reached in two, but only after a strong line had been taken: the pack animals and their drivers were discharged and it was decided to take the risk of being able to replace them at a neighbouring village.

And the task which lay before them? It was not likely to prove a simple and straightforward matter. They had to find Everest in the first place, and, having found it, to explore each of the valleys which wound up to the foot of the central pile. Before this could be attempted the men had to be trained for moving safely on steep snow or ice, and in the management of ice-axe and rope. After a fortnight of preliminary work ' I cut a staircase slanting up to a small island of rock 100 feet away; from that security I began to bring the party up. We had now the interesting experience of seeing our coolies for the first time on real hard ice; it was not a convincing spectacle, as they made their way up with the ungainly movements of beginners; and though the last man never left the secure anchorage of the *bergschrund*, the proportion of two sahibs to five coolies seemed

THE RECONNAISSANCE AND ASSAULT

lamentably weak; and when one man slipped from the steep steps at an awkward corner, though Bullock was able to hold him, it was clearly time to retire.' It is astonishing that with no verbal communication they were able so to train these men as safe mountaineers that the whole reconnaissance, which involved high climbing extending over a period of three months, was achieved without a single mishap.

The valleys which they were setting out to explore were separated by high ridges which made lateral communication extremely difficult, while the scale on which they were formed may be gathered from the fact that the surfaces of the glaciers which flowed down them appeared in the distance like a sea of little ice pinnacles, and each pinnacle on a close approach proved to be an ice tower 40 to 50 feet high. The aim of the reconnaissance was a correct understanding of the whole form and structure of the mountain, and a detailed knowledge of the accessibility of all the faces and arêtes of which it was formed. This is an easy thing to picture now it is done, but in the doing it was like asking an ant to make a plan of a cathedral: each obstacle surmounted reveals a new embarrassment of colossal proportions, and bird's-eye views, except in a very limited degree, are unobtainable.

The work of this first expedition, less concentrated and less dramatic, was yet of far greater extent than that of subsequent years, both in time and space. For the later attempts the one and only feasible route was known and planned beforehand, and the

EVEREST

actual work of organizing the high camps and making the assault was a matter of five or six weeks. In 1921 it was just three months from the time when Mallory and Bullock established their first advanced camp on the Rongbuk Glacier to the day, September 25th, when they were beaten back by wind and snow from the North Col. After a month spent among the western approaches of the great massif, during which they were able to establish the fact that no assault on that side could hope for success, the climbing party made an immense detour and attacked the high fortress from the east, at a point about 16 miles, as the crow flies, from their previous glacier camp; this immense distance being the diameter of the great central bulk of Everest and its attendant glaciers above 16,000 feet.

A fortnight's exploration of the eastern approaches sufficed to confirm the opinion already formed, that the only feasible point of attack was from the North Col, the high saddle which formed the barrier between their two centres of exploration lying roughly at the centre of the 16 miles between the Kharta Glacier and their previous high camp.

Before the third and final stage—the assault, the whole company foregathered for ten days' rest in comfort at Kharta. During this interval the weather was their chief anxiety. The season was getting late and snow fell daily. After a move had been made on August 31st to the advanced base at 17,300 feet the party had to wait there three weeks before any further advance was possible. During all this time Mallory was taking anxious note of the physical con-

North-western aspect of Everest from the Rongbuk glacier

THE RECONNAISSANCE AND ASSAULT

dition of the party. It was clear that the strain was beginning to tell. He himself, before the rest at Kharta, had had to lie up two days with swollen glands and a sore throat, and though he had so far recovered as to be able at the advanced camp still to go up about 1,500 feet in an hour he notes that he began to experience 'a certain lack of exuberance when going uphill', and to realize that his reserve of strength had somehow diminished. As for the rest, three of the strongest coolies were ill at the advanced camp, and of the sahibs 'at least it must be said that several of them were not looking their best'.

Mallory's attitude towards this final stage of the expedition is brought out clearly in two letters which I shall quote below. The first was written on September 9th, during the wait at the advanced camp, the second during the voyage home. The next move was a deliberate attempt to climb the mountain, or rather to test the possibility of it. How forlorn the chances were, with such a party and under such conditions, we now know; but it must be remembered that, having found the only possible route to the top, no reconnaissance would have been complete without an exploration of the route up to the limit of their powers. That Mallory could plan a supreme effort and all the time retain the balanced judgement of a mountaineer will be clear from his own words. 'I've just received your letter with six weeks' mails which were hung up in Tibet—sitting patiently on the edge of a flood. How wonderful, I can't help exclaiming, that it should just come at this moment

EVEREST

when the assault is all prepared and only waiting for the weather. Long before you get this you will know the result, which may make my speculations look foolish; but I must make them; I can think of nothing else. The excitement of reconnaissance is all over—it *was* exciting—and we have found a good way to approach the mountain. That last push to a snow col, which we had to see over, was the biggest effort I have ever made on a mountain. The whole thing is on my shoulders—I can say that to you— Bullock follows well and is safe; but you know what it means on a long exhausting effort to lead all the time, and snow shoes in deep snow on a steep slope are no small added burden. Height tells too, but I think rather less than people imagine. I can still do 1,500 feet an hour undistressed (and also unladen) at least up to 20,000, as I found before breakfast this morning; and the other day up to our col about 23,000 we were doing what would have taken the wind of any party in the Alps. It's all a question of lungs; in the penultimate stage one breathes as hard and deep as possible, once out and in for each step; and after that it becomes necessary to halt after a few steps and acquire a sort of potential energy by breathing to carry one on again. But of course the laden coolie loses power much more rapidly as he gets up and the first part of our present problem is to get him high enough. It's no use attempting the carrying over three stages on snow until it hardens; we're simply waiting for the weather—and the longer we have to wait the colder it will be. Our 1st advanced camp at 20,000 feet is on stones where

THE RECONNAISSANCE AND ASSAULT

we can burn wood, and everything we shall want is waiting there except what we can carry up with us. From there we shall go to our col of the other day, or somewhere near it, easy enough going up a glacier once the conditions are right. Our 3rd camp will be at about 24,000, I hope somewhere near what we call the "North Col" between Everest and the first peak on its North ridge—an easy stage. It's an easy slope up from there to a great shoulder of the NE. arête which must be 27,000 feet or thereabouts, and from there to the summit there should be no obstacle unless on the steep final up, which looks all too formidable. Naturally much depends upon how high we can get the coolies up from the "North Col" on the 3rd day from our 1st camp. And we have still to find a place where a tent can be pitched. If we can get them up 2,000 feet from the Col we shall have a chance I believe, a bare outside chance perhaps, of crawling to the top.

'Morshead and Wheeler are both joining us for the assault. M. is wonderfully stouthearted, but has not the lungs for this job I fear. Wheeler hasn't been out with us yet, but as his stomach is out of order as often as not, I don't expect much of him. If they don't come on from the final camp I shall take coolies; one or two of them are wonderful good goers.

'It's a pleasure to tell you something of my plans —you'll appreciate how much they mean on this occasion. I hope you'll bear to have them thrust upon you. Lord, how I wish you were here to talk it all over. It has been rather a strain, altogether.

EVEREST

I was unfortunate in having an attack of tonsillitis just before we finished our reconnaissance and I feel somehow I'm not so strong as I was—less reserve somehow. Altogether it's a trying time while we wait here and try and keep the coolies happy, and I begin to feel that sort of malaise one has before putting a great matter to the touch. At what point am I going to stop? It's going to be a fearfully difficult decision; there's an incalculable element about other men's physical condition, and all the more so under these strange conditions. I almost hope I shall be the first to give out!

'Well, that's as much as you'll tolerate about my feelings. We've received the news to-day of the truce in Ireland—which makes me feel more like praying than anything almost I can remember. I shan't be sorry to get back to civilization and know again what's going on in the world; it's a poor world perhaps but it remains interesting even here—if only as a contrast to Tibet, which is a hateful country inhabited by hateful people. The great mountains give their flashes of beauty; Makalu is indescribably impressive; but on the whole they are disappointing and infinitely less beautiful than the Alps.'

Although Mallory was not the first to give out, the decision to retreat, as it happened, was not so difficult to make. The party consisting of Wheeler, Bullock, three coolies and himself reached the North Col for the first time at 11.30 a.m. on September 24th. 'By this time two coolies were distinctly tired, though by no means incapable of coming on; the third, who had been in front, was comparatively fresh. Wheeler thought he might be good for some further effort, but had lost all feeling in his feet. Bullock was tired, but by sheer will power would evidently come on—how far, one couldn't say. For my part, I had had the wonderful good fortune of sleeping tolerably well at both high camps and now finding my best form; I supposed I might be capable of another 2,000 feet, and there would be no time for more. But what lay ahead of us? My eyes had often strayed, as we came up, to the rounded edge above the col and the final rocks below the northeast arête. If ever we had doubted whether the arête was accessible, it was impossible to doubt any longer. For a long way up these easy rock and snow slopes there was neither danger nor difficulty. But at present there was wind. Even where we stood under the lee of a little ice cliff it came in fierce gusts at frequent intervals, blowing up the powdery snow. On the Col beyond it was blowing a gale. And higher was a more fearful sight. The powdery fresh snow was being swept along in unbroken spindrift, and the very ridge where our route lay was marked out to receive its unmitigated fury. . . . To see, in fact, was enough; the wind had settled the question; it would have been folly to go on. Nevertheless, some little discussion took place as to what might be possible, and we struggled a few steps further to put the matter to the test. For a few moments we exposed ourselves on the Col to feel the full strength of the blast, then struggled back to shelter. Nothing more was said about pushing our assault any further.

EVEREST

'It remained to make a final decision on the morning of the 25th. We were evidently too weak a party to play a waiting game at this altitude. We must either take our camp to the Col or go back.... The crucial matter was the condition of the climbers. Were we fit to push the adventure further? ... And what more were we likely to accomplish from a camp on Chang La? The second night had been no less windy than the first.... The only signs of a change now pointed to no improvement, but rather to a heavy fall of snow—by no means an improbable event according to local lore. The arguments, in fact, were all on one side; it would be bad heroics to take wrong risks; and fairly facing the situation one could only admit the necessity of retreat.'[1]

The story of this first attempt may fittingly be closed by the vivid touches of the next letter written as he was approaching Marseilles. 'I think it was disappointment more than anything else that prevented me writing before—the terrible difference between my visions of myself with a few determined spirits setting forth from our perched camp on that high pass, crawling up at least to a much higher point where the summit itself would seem almost within reach, and coming down tired but not dispirited—satisfied, rather, just with the effort; and on the other hand the reality as we found it, the blown snow endlessly swept over the grey slopes —just the grim prospect, no respite and no hope.

'Well, that mood has passed long ago, and now, after writing my report for the Alpine Club, I'm

[1] *Mount Everest. The Reconnaissance*, 1921, pp. 259–61.

THE RECONNAISSANCE AND ASSAULT

conscious of the only feeling that slept: thank God it was like that, with no temptation to go on. We came back without accident, not even a frost-bitten toe; it seems now a question not as to what might have happened higher, but what *would* have happened with unfailing certainty; it was a pitiful party at the last, not fit to be on a mountain-side anywhere.

'I can't tell the story at present; I've been writing too much about the whole business, and it all seems to hinge on complicated details of organization; they *will* obtrude themselves. A few scenes are unforgettable;—the party straggling up to Windy Gap—this was two days before we used the camp there; Morshead and I looked down as we were approaching the pass; we were all stragglers, ones and twos in the tracks all the way down that final slope, and lower still a lone figure huddled up on the snow. I don't know how they managed to struggle up with their loads in that powdery stuff; but somehow the loads reached the pass, 11 out of 14. It was about the gamest thing I've seen, and secured for us our small success in the end.

'And then the camp on the pass two days later—Bury, and Wollaston, all the lot of us there except Raeburn. I got up last, except Wollaston, very tired—I wasn't fit that day; and there were the rest sitting under the rim, the best shelter that could be found, and shuddering in the dry smother of snow blown up by every gust; there was a suggestion of going down to encamp on the other side, which I resisted; then the tents were pitched, and each crawled into his hole. In a few minutes all was still. We were at very close quarters, seven tents I think in the little shallow snow-basin; but hardly a remark passed from one to another. No cooking, no hand stirred for a thought of comfort; only rest, not sweet but deathlike, as though the spirit of the party had died within it. And so it had, we buried it next morning.

'At the last camp, under the North Col, we spent two nights; an unforgettable place too—I'll show you a photograph one of these days. It might have been an endless stretch of snow about us, it was so flat and the world was so big; but at the same time the great cliffs on three sides of us were a felt presence. And down there, we were at the bottom of something; the wind found us out; there was never a more determined and bitter enemy. Two wild nights, and two mornings chilled by the shadow of defeat.

'Nothing very remarkable remains in my mind about the ascent to the North Col, except perhaps Wheeler's black beard coming up behind me. I seem to know too well the form and angle of a particular snow slope; I must have looked up a great number of times as we traversed it; there was a reason for that. And as we reached the Col I was aware of the devil, dancing in a sudden turbillion of snow which took away my breath. . . . But I shall never end if I recall every little impression like that. One scene would have amused you: On the return journey we reached Windy Gap in what seemed like a blizzard, though it was really only blown snow once again. The men stood gasping, unable to go on at the very moment of reaching it, and I tugged in vain; then

THE RECONNAISSANCE AND ASSAULT

they tried to shelter under the rim on the site of our camp. As they stood with their backs to the wind I drew their attention to a number of loads left there by the other party. Suddenly with one will we dragged them to the edge, hurled them down the slope, and stood there laughing like children as we watched them roll and roll, 600 or 700 feet down.'

In seven and a half months from the date of this retreat Mallory was back on the same spot with the second expedition. But in circumstances how very different! The parties of climbers on this second attempt were backed up by a large and well-equipped organization—when the expedition reached the base camp on May 1st there were no less than 300 baggage animals, 20 ponies, 60 hired coolies, and 100 or so other Tibetans of varying degrees of usefulness. The matter of speech, too, was a handicap no longer, for three of the officers of the expedition were perfectly able to deal directly with the men and with the people of the country.

There is no doubt that under the new conditions Mallory was optimistic as to the chances of reaching the summit. He had had his days of depression in 1921, when he could write, during the first month of exploration of the western approaches. 'I sometimes think of this expedition as a fraud from beginning to end invented by the wild enthusiasm of one man—Younghusband, puffed up by the would-be wisdom of certain pundits in the Alpine Club, and imposed upon the youthful ardour of your humble servant. Certainly the reality must be strangely

EVEREST

different from their dream. The long imagined snow slopes of this Northern face of Everest with their gentle and inviting angle turn out to be the most appalling precipice, nearly 10,000 feet high. . . . The prospect of ascent in any direction is about nil and our present job is to rub our noses against the impossible in such a way as to persuade mankind that some noble heroism has failed once again. And the heroism at present consists in enduring the discomforts of a camp at 19,000 feet in the company of a band, of whose native tongue I can scarcely understand a syllable, and in urging these good folk to rise before daylight in the most usually vain hope that by the time we have got somewhere something may still remain unhidden by the clouds. . . . Believe about one-quarter of this mood and supply the others which are beyond me to describe—from your sympathy. . . . The rucksack is packed with tomorrow's provisions; the compass and glasses and aneroid are to hand waiting for the start; and I must to bed soon with the alarm watch under my pillow . . . the snow? It's a passing shower, we hope, we hope. The peaks will be clear and glorious in the morning.'

In some such way as this the moods had alternated during the journey home and the months in England. 'The enterprise is so desperate', he had written during the journey home, 'that it's barely worth while trying again and anyway not without eight first-rate climbers; they can't get eight, certainly not soon, perhaps not even the year after. They already want to know whether I'll go again; when they press

THE RECONNAISSANCE AND ASSAULT

for an answer I shall tell them they can get the other seven first. . . . I wouldn't go again next year, as the saying is, for all the gold in Arabia—and later, well, I must have time to look round.' Nevertheless he did start again, with no more than three desperately overworked months in England, during which he had to write his contribution to the printed book in the scanty intervals of a lecturing programme. And, once started, he was full of lively enthusiasm for the project, a state of mind which was fostered by the happy personal relationships existing among the party. 'I am enjoying this venture hugely,' he wrote from Sikkim. 'It's the jolliest party, and everything is well arranged. The General is being perfectly splendid. He is making heroic exertions to get rid of his tummy, and walked nearly the whole way up yesterday, a rise of 5,500 feet. It was rather exhilarating to feel the high keen air again and to sleep above 12,000 feet. . . . Norton is one of the best—extraordinarily keen and active and full of interest, and gentle and charming withal. He is to be my stable companion, I understand, and I don't doubt I shall like him in that capacity as well as any one—but I would have said the same of Somervell or Geoffrey Bruce, while Morshead is naturally more my friend than any one, so you may judge how happy I find myself in my companions. Noel is full of activity with his cinematograph and photography. He was very pleased with a film of me bathing; he was waiting with his apparatus in a valley to take the animals crossing a bridge. Norton, Bruce, and I came down in front of them, and as I was very hot I proceeded straight to the stream, took off my shirt and immersed the upper part of my body, and, in fact, had an excellent wash, as presumably all the world will be able to see—at all events I shall have a testimonial for cleanliness.'

It will be remembered that the expedition was equipped with compressed oxygen for use in the high climbing, but it was not to be used on the first attempt, and it fell to Mallory's lot to be one of this first party. That, I know, was as he would have wished. He had always a strong feeling for keeping the whole adventure within what he regarded as the bounds of legitimate mountaineering, and if the summit could not be reached without adventitious aid I doubt whether, in his heart of hearts, he felt it should be reached at all. Something of this attitude he expressed afterwards in his printed contribution to the story of the assault. ' It is true ', he says, ' that I did what I could to reach the summit, but now as I look back and see all those wonderful preparations, the great array of boxes collected at Phari Dzong and filling up the courtyard of the bungalow, the train of animals and coolies carrying our baggage across Tibet, the thirteen selected Europeans so snugly wrapt in their woollen waistcoats and Jaeger pants, their armour of wind-proof materials, their splendid overcoats, the furred finneskoes or felt-sided boots or fleece-lined moccasins devised to keep warm their feet, and the sixty strong porters with them delighting in underwear from England and leathern jerkins and puttees from Kashmir; and then, unforgettable scene, the scatter of our stores

THE RECONNAISSANCE AND ASSAULT

at the base camp, the innumerable neatly made wooden boxes concealing the rows and rows of tins —of Harris's sausages, Hunter's hams, Heinz's spaghetti, herrings *soi-disant* fresh, sardines, sliced bacon, peas, beans, and a whole forgotten host besides, sauce-bottles for the Mess tables, and the rare bottles more precious than these, the gay tins of sweet biscuits, Ginger Nuts and Rich Mixed, and all the carefully chosen delicacies; and besides all these for our sustenance or pleasure, the fuel supply, uncovered in the centre of the camp, green and blue two-gallon-cans of paraffin and petrol, and an impressive heap of yak-dung; and the climbing equipment—the gay little tents with crimson flies or yellow, pitched here only to be seen and admired, the bundles of soft sleeping-bags, soft as eiderdown quilt can be, the ferocious crampons and other devices, steel-pointed and terrible, for boots' armament, the business-like coils of rope, the little army of steel cylinders containing oxygen under high pressure, and, not least, the warlike sets of apparatus for using the life-giving gas; and lastly, when I call to mind the whole begoggled crowd moving with slow determination over the snow and up the mountain slopes and with such remarkable persistence bearing up the formidable loads, when after the lapse of months I envisage the whole prodigious evidences of this vast intention, how can I help rejoicing in the yet undimmed splendour, the undiminished glory, the unconquered supremacy of Mount Everest?'[1]

[1] *Mount Everest, The Assault*, 1922, pp. 123–4.

EVEREST

Apart from the elaborate organization, conditions this year differed widely from those of the reconnaissance the year before. That had extended from the end of June until the end of September, following on the heels of the monsoon. This year it had been decided to make the assault before the coming of the monsoon, for then the rocky slopes above the North Col would be much more clear of snow; and it seemed probable, too, that this plan would give the best chance of a spell, although a short one, of warm and quiet weather.

A new condition to be reckoned with, however, was now that of time. The arrival of the monsoon, although normally to be expected in the first half of June might be heralded by earlier snowfalls. Extreme cold would preclude high climbing earlier in the year than the middle of May. So that the attempt had to be timed for the second half of May and early June. After the arrival of the whole expedition at the base camp on May 1st, the establishment of the higher camps took longer than had been anticipated owing to the defection of the large party of Tibetan porters after two days' work. May is the ploughing time in Tibet, and even the high pay would not induce them to leave their fields for longer. As a result it was not until May 20th that the first assault upon the mountain was launched. For this first attempt without oxygen, in the company of Somervell, Norton, and Morshead, Mallory was full of enthusiasm, although he did not expect, weather conditions being what they were, to reach the top. 'The difficulties, in all human probability, will be

Mallory and Norton at near 27,000 feet

THE RECONNAISSANCE AND ASSAULT

such as we know', he wrote just before the start. 'Our endurance and will to go on taking precautions are less known factors, but with such good people as these are I feel sure that we shall all be anxious to help each other and that, after all, provided we are competent mountaineers, is the great safeguard.

'I have very good hopes with the coolies fit and cheerful that we shall establish a camp well above Chang La the day after to-morrow—you realize I expect that Norton and Morshead have joined, so we, the four of us, will be sleeping at the North Col to-morrow night and we hope about 25,000 the following night—and then!

'I can't say that I feel stronger for the days here (21,000 feet), or weaker either for that matter. Somervell says he went better up to Chang La yesterday than on the 13th. Well—it's all on the knees of the gods, and they are bare cold knees. We shan't get to the top; if we reach the shoulder at 27,400 it will be better than any one here expects.'

In spite of a burst of excessive cold and the sickness of five out of their nine porters, so that all reserves were lost before they had taken a step from the North Col, the party achieved their magnificent climb of 26,985 feet. As one reads Mallory's account of this affair it is no mere question of figures which impresses one, but the fact that it was carried through from start to finish as a piece of first-rate mountaineering. There was a slip, it is true, on the descent; but their recovery was one of the best things of the day. They were moving across a snow slope, Mallory in front; one man slipped, and in a twinkling first one and then the other of the men behind him were pulled from their steps. One might scarcely realize, reading the quiet account of the affair, that they were all within an ace of repeating the tragedy to Whymper's party on the first ascent of the Matterhorn; but in the second of time before the strain came, without turning to see what had happened, Mallory had driven in his axe and belayed the rope round it. Rope and belay held firm, and in another minute, in spite of their eight or nine hours climbing, following on a night at 25,000 feet, the whole party was moving down again safely. The descent was completed without mishap, although it took another seven hours, and they had to find their way in darkness among the seracs of the North Col without even a lantern.

The continued bad weather, following on this gruelling experience and the failure of the oxygen party to reach the top, seems to have altered Mallory's whole attitude, for the time, towards further attempts. In physical powers both Somervell and he recovered fairly quickly; but from enthusiasm he had passed to a dogged determination. ' It is delightful to hear about it all ', he wrote to me on June 1st in reply to a letter describing our petty exploits nearer home, ' although I am almost painfully reminded that there are pleasures in the high endeavour of mountaineering—this sentiment comes naturally on the eve of another attempt on Everest. You'll have read my account of the first and Finch's of the second. The mountain has taken his toll among us;

THE RECONNAISSANCE AND ASSAULT

but, Lord! How much worse it might have been! No coolies frostbitten to speak of—almost a miracle when one considers that a party were sent up from the North Col at 4 p.m. to Finch's high camp and got in again at 11 p.m.... David, it's an infernal mountain, cold and treacherous. Frankly the game is not good enough. The risks of getting caught are too great; the margin of strength when men are at great heights is too small. Perhaps it's mere folly to go up again. But how can I be out of the hunt? And then, given the right weather, there's quite a good chance of reaching the top, at all events with oxygen. We've learnt something too, and I have good hopes of preserving toes and fingers, though almost infinite care is required. Our climb was a pretty killing affair. Norton as well as Morshead is clean out of it now; Morshead will lose a toe besides six finger tips; poor man, I'm awfully sorry about it; but he won't be incapacitated in any way. It sounds more like war than sport, and perhaps it is. Lord! How I long for a green thing or two in this vale of stones! On what a day to be writing to England, while one sees here nothing but the inimical snows and the endless debris of gaunt rock masses. The compensations are to be found in the party—a lovely lot of men in all, and nothing could have been better that way than our climb. I'm very happy in spite of these laments.'

There would be no value in going over again here the details of that last attempt which ended in disaster, when the whole party was swept down by an avalanche and seven of the porters lost their lives. Of the wisdom of undertaking it Mallory speaks fully in a long letter written to Geoffrey Young, which is given below. The letter is valuable in another way. There must always be a temptation, when writing, at a later date, of an event for which blame may rest for lack of precautions taken, to allow the emphasis to become warped and to insist on the unforeseeable nature of the catastrophe. In this intimate letter, written immediately after the event, and in which he takes the whole blame upon himself, the account of the facts agrees exactly with that written months later on for publication. 'I am quite knocked out by this accident', he wrote from the base camp. 'Seven of these brave men killed, and they were ignorant of mountain dangers, like children in our care. And I'm to blame. So you wouldn't expect much sense. But I want to tell you something about it.

'I suppose the whole plan of making another attempt once the first burst of the monsoon had brought heavy snow is open to criticism. Actually we left this camp on June 3rd with the clouds still threatening. The snow came on the following night and day, and during the long day we spent at Camp 1 I thought out my position. Of course if we had come back saying that the snow made Everest impracticable and that now the monsoon had come it was time to go home—no one would have said a word against our decision. But it seemed to me not unreasonable to expect a break of fine weather, as there was last year, before the monsoon set in continuously, and that in some balance between the old fierce west wind and the monsoon current we should have a

THE RECONNAISSANCE AND ASSAULT

calm day and our chance at last; at all events the proper ending would be to be turned back by some definite danger or difficulty on the mountain, or to be beaten by height as before—I have little doubt, besides, that using oxygen and given the opportunity, Somervell and I would have reached the top —for whatever that performance might be worth.

'On the 5th we went up in clouds and intermittent snow to Camp 3. On the 6th all rested there in glorious warmth and sunshine. As you may remember a steep slope has to be crossed below the shelf on which our North Col Camp is established; but the snow solidifies with wonderful rapidity and I reckoned that, with fine weather, it would probably be safe to cross it on the 8th. Meanwhile we could establish tracks so far and get the hard work done. The first part of the ascent had previously been a steep ice-slope; when we started upon the 7th it provided a test of the snow—and the snow was binding so well that we made new tracks up it without cutting steps (about 10.30 a.m., so that the slope had had five hours' sun). Above, the slopes are comparatively gentle and except in one place, where a dozen steps had to be cut, we had previously found good snow. The new snow was up to our knees but binding well, not a powdery substance. No one of us three had an inkling of danger or the thought of an avalanche on such easy slopes. The avalanche started from under some ice cliffs not far above us on the left; it was not of the sort that peels a whole slope; looking at the debris afterwards I conjectured that the snow under the cliffs had had less sun and remained powdery; at all events it was lying at a steeper angle and had sufficient weight to push down the lower snow; but the whole slide was only about 200 feet on the average—a very small affair to have such fatal consequences; the trouble was the ice cliff below and the fall of from 40 feet to 60 feet must have killed most of the men at once.

'Thinking it all out with wisdom after the event I come back simply to my ignorance, to generalizations on too little observation, and the lifetime it requires to know all about it. But I also remember Donald Robertson and the great sleeping ones that have but to stir in their slumber. And perhaps you'll remember that for me. At all events you won't believe we were pushing recklessly on; and the story, I think, does not accuse us of being careless of coolies' lives; we three were in front to take turns in making the track.

'The bitterness is partly in the irony of fate. Somervell and I had had experience enough of Everest to feel that one must take no chances with that mountain. I was never so resolved to be careful, and half our talk had been how to ensure the safety of the coolies —perhaps you don't realize that at one time they had been going up and down unconducted and unroped, a party of them actually arriving among the crevasses of the North Col in that state at 11 p.m.—and perhaps we were a little consciously virtuous in condemning this example and resolving to arrange otherwise.

'Do you know that sickening feeling that one can't go back and have it undone, and that nothing will make good?

THE RECONNAISSANCE AND ASSAULT

'I don't much care what the world says, but I care very much what you and a few others think. I shall be home before the end of August. I shan't feel much like showing my face, but I would like to see yours before too long, so let me know when you will be in the South.'

VII

EVEREST: THE LAST ADVENTURE

IT fell to Mallory's lot after each of the first two expeditions to play the part of the chief showman and to give the lectures which must needs help to pay the bill for the undertaking. He had a good voice and manner, and at any rate after the second expedition the lectures were a great success. The year before they had been unequal, the narrative vigorous and effective, but with some prepared portions rather metaphysical and poetical, with a straining after pictorial effect which he did not ' get across '. From the very first, even at the original meeting of welcome in the Queen's Hall, the easy and natural tones of his voice could be heard everywhere without effort.

He had certainly achieved a more eminent platform than the one in his classroom, and he thoroughly enjoyed his opportunities upon it. ' Everest has been rather a good lark ', he wrote after the first expedition, ' and not least perhaps the lecturing. I'm very much " on tour " at present, like some celebrated *prima donna* in the provinces. I've given seventeen lectures, I find, in the last three weeks, and now that it has become a habit to appear on the boards each evening I find my vocal activities there no greater effort than singing in my bath—indeed they give me a very similar satisfaction. I am much intrigued by the whole art of casting a spell upon an audience; it's rather amusing to practise one's guile on two or three thousand expectant persons, but I wonder if the experience will ever be related to anything more useful in the future?'

From January to April 1923 a lecture tour was arranged in America, and he went through all the usual mill of pressmen and photographers. ' Here's a specimen of American advertisement. General view of G. M. sitting at open window on the 10th floor, gazing down into Vth Avenue. On Wednesday afternoon I had four pressmen in here. I had already been rehearsed in what I should say, but I don't know that that made much difference—I sent them away happy and the puffs duly appeared next morning. But that is not all. These first puffs have to be backed up by subsequent paragraphs, and so I had a long talk with a young man who circulates to the press information about this hotel's distinguished visitors; he wanted to get a " contrast in value " he said! And to this end he wished me to say that the great mountaineers of the Expedition were all men of scientific eminence, or that mental training had more to do with the matter than physique. Can you imagine anything more childish?—but I expect that is just what Americans are—boyish. New York itself often gives the impression of a splendid gesture against a background of emptiness. Each individual skyscraper is making its own gesture rather than being part of a whole street; and, as you see their silhouettes against the sky, they are all playing a part in a grotesque world of toy giants. The important streets give me an utterly different feeling from those in an English town chiefly because the buildings have such very different heights, and don't appear closely ranged side to side, but stand up separately (though of course the bases of them are side by side) with dark shadows between. The disparity of monsters and dwarfs reminds me of the illustrations to *Gulliver's Travels*. The spear-head of skyscrapers lying on a tongue of land which one approaches coming up the river is much more of an architectural whole, and is one of the most wonderful effects of piled up mass I have ever seen. They can build sometimes—the Public Library in Vth Avenue, a comparatively low building, is very good indeed; and the absence of Gothic and its derivatives is such a relief! '

Mallory had had great hopes of this American tour, and was disappointed when he arrived in New York to find how few lectures had been arranged. He had, however, very appreciative audiences, after that of the first lecture, in Washington, which appears from the next letter to have been a frost. ' I've been very busy with the lecture, much more work than you would suppose, cutting out one scrap and another, making a new beginning, and a new end, incorporating Somervell's slides and about ten showing the reconnaissance—and, most important of all, winnowing it all over to get the expression better for an American audience. And in the end this afternoon they were the most unresponsive crowd I ever talked to—never a clap when I meant them to applaud, and almost never a laugh. They weren't

THE LAST ADVENTURE

comfortable with me, I don't know why. But they *were* held, just. And afterwards much handshaking and kind words as though it had been a grand success. I believe they were just like the Torquay audience, only kinder.

'And this evening it came right off from the first word to the last, I did what I liked with them; they took all my points; it was technically better than any lecture I've ever given either year and had any amount of spontaneity too. There, if it doesn't " take " now—well, I can do no more, and I'll come home.'

At his first lecture in New York the Broadhurst Theatre was only half full, and he feared that the Washington experience was going to be repeated. 'However I had friends in the audience—amongst them *all* the members of the American Alpine Club who had been present at the dinner they gave me, so I didn't worry. I got them all right at the start and they proved quite a pleasant, appreciative audience —they really went away *fizzing* and I had reports of nice things said as they were going out—so that was all right. I must tell you that Poel who has a highly critical knowledge of the stage said he hadn't a single hint to give me, and he didn't see how it could be better. I was really pleased to hear that from him. But the whole importance of this lecture was to have a good press, and when I read the papers at breakfast there was almost nothing. The *New York Times* had a large heading and one-third of a column, but the whole thing was turned into Anti-Prohibition propaganda. However, the

Tribune came out with a very good and sympathetic report—and that may do what is wanted. There is no doubt people over here are really impressed by the story, and I shall feel that the lectures have been worth while, even though the number remains small for the time spent in the country.'

In spite of the success of individual lectures, the number which had been arranged was too small to make the tour a great success financially, and in consequence Mallory was feeling a good deal depressed about the future on the voyage home; more especially at the prospect of having to lecture daily with the cinematograph film in London after his return. 'I can't tell you how I hate the thought of this, which seems just a dead job. And there goes the spring I had hoped to be spending at home. But now that I come back with so little I simply can't afford to chuck away chances of making some money with so little effort. Isn't it a dilemma to make a man swear? Question—whether the continuous humdrum which brings each day a known task with it, and at the end of so many days the definite prospect of so many workless days to follow, isn't a vastly preferable lot to this topsy-turvy life of mine, half of it spent away from the surroundings I most want. In short, why don't I go back to be a model schoolmaster?' He escaped the film lecturing, happily, and very soon after his return there occurred the possibility of settled work in Cambridge. The Board of Extra-Mural Studies were in need of an assistant secretary and lecturer, and to the great rejoicing of his Cambridge friends Mallory was appointed to the post. It was the happiest solution. The project of the new school, for financial and other reasons, had slipped into the background, and I doubt whether he could in any case have settled down happily to that after the two expeditions to Everest. His interest in the growing human being had by now become concentrated upon his own three children, and his experience of lecturing to large audiences, with conspicuous success, had developed in him a taste for influencing large masses of people; and he wanted something more intellectually independent, more mature than the boyish mind, to lay his mind fairly alongside of. In this new work both as a teacher and as an organizer of new enterprises I believe he was very successful. He had the prestige of his exploits, for one thing, and besides that he had learned to meet strangers with an equable courtesy; he had never been a respecter of persons, and his eagerness and charm were at the service of all whom he met.

It was very noticeable at this time what a big change had come to him with the later years. The perfect equability which he had always shown as a climber had taken a deeper hold, so that his charm of appearance and temperament became no longer a separate quality, but the inevitable expression of the whole man himself. He seemed to have developed quite a new kind of serenity, and to have sloughed off his old impatience, his hatred of caution and stupidity, and to have developed a gentleness and sympathy which were all the more effective because they were so transparently sincere. It was not that he had parted with the fire of youth; he was as eager as ever, and even more enthusiastic, but it was the transformation of the easy-going rather heedless youth into the complete and courteous man. As a host he was delightful. He had plenty to say, but he neglected no one, never kept the talk in his own hands but unobtrusively gave every one the chance of taking his or her share. At the same time his sympathy for different types of character expanded very much. In old days he had enthusiastically admired or frankly contemned. Now he seemed to be able to find people of quite opposite views and temperament to his own interesting and amusing. In talk and argument he seemed to have parted altogether with the old contentious and disdainful style. He was extremely good natured and gave every one's arguments full weight. It was an instructive change, for he never had a dry regard or respect for social duty in itself; duty was always an active motion of his mind towards something that he recognized as, or suspected of being, ultimately beautiful. His features reflected the change, for in losing their extreme youthfulness they had become more firm and clearly marked, the whole expression being that of a character more tolerant without letting go of its own ideals, and more sympathetic because more sure of itself.

When the question arose of a third attempt upon Everest the situation was, for Mallory, profoundly different from the two previous occasions. He had recently embarked upon a new, intricate, and important job which was likely to go on expanding;

THE LAST ADVENTURE

and then also, to leave his wife and children as comparative strangers in Cambridge, only just settled into their new house, was a prospect very different from that when he could think of them in Godalming, where Mrs. Mallory had lived all her life and with her father and sister as near neighbours.

From the other aspect, too, the undertaking wore a very different complexion. The first reconnaissance of the mountain, in 1921, I think he had thoroughly enjoyed. His part in the expedition of the following year was the inevitable sequel to his own pioneer work of exploration. It was unthinkable that he should not be there, with his unique experience, for the first great attack upon the summit. But in 1924 all this was changed. There was no longer the stimulus of adventure into unknown country and among strange peoples, nor could he hope to enjoy it as mountaineering. After the first attempt of 1922, and before the avalanche had carried seven porters to their death, he had already begun to doubt whether the risks did not go beyond those of reasonable mountaineering. ' It sounds more like war than sport', he had written, ' and perhaps it is . . . but how can I be out of the hunt? ' It would be wrong to think of the sequel as the tragedy of a man going out unwillingly and losing his life. But it is important that as true an impression as may be should be given of Mallory's own feelings towards the question of his final adventure. This is the more difficult since his feelings were naturally mixed. The strongest forces urged him both to stay and to go: the closest ties of family and affection, and the responsibilities and interest of his work in Cambridge; against this the question, how could he be out of the hunt? It was a call to the highest and greatest endeavour in mountaineering that the world could provide, and what he had attempted out there was still to do. But more than this, if his experience of the two previous years would make for the final success of the expedition, either through himself or others, then it was not in his nature to stand aside from an attempt which called for the highest use of all those faculties of endurance, leadership, and mountain-craft which had been growing and strengthening during twenty years.

As regards the actual decision he told me beforehand that the line he should take would be to leave it wholly in the hands of others. If the Everest Committee applied to the Board under whom he worked at Cambridge, and if the latter acquiesced in his going, he was ready to go; but he decided to make no application himself, nor to influence any decision by making known his own wishes.

My impression of his state of mind—and it is to be taken as no more than my personal opinion—is that he would have been profoundly relieved if the whole expedition had been called off; but that in any other event he felt it as inevitable, and indeed he wished, to be there. He did not really *want* to go. Of course he felt it would be great fun if they succeeded, but he did not strongly believe in the possibility; or rather he knew that this depended on the coincidence of so many favourable conditions that a further attempt, for him, was hardly justified. The

THE LAST ADVENTURE

Everest Committee were urgent that he should go, however, and the Board acquiesced with scarcely any discussion; they no doubt felt that if he were to succeed it would give him a prestige which would undoubtedly be of great advantage to him in his work. When the decision had been made for him in this way he was once more happy and optimistic. ' A line to let you know I'm going once more', he wrote to Geoffrey Young. ' Not the slightest opposition from the Board here. But a big tug for me with the ends of a new job gathering in my hands ; and Ruth will feel it more this time too. I'm very happy it is decided so.'

The last weeks before his departure were a desperate rush. Besides the work in his office he was giving two courses of evening classes, each some thirty miles away from Cambridge, and all these occupations he carried on up to the very day of his starting. Every half-hour of daylight seemed to be taken up and, motoring to and from his classes at Raunds and Halstead, after starting about four o'clock, he did not get home till eleven o'clock at night. It happened that Mr. William Nicholson was just then in Cambridge, painting a portrait of the Master of Trinity, and he expressed a wish to ' record ' Mallory, as he said, before he went. I tried to arrange a few sittings, but the thing seemed almost impossible: two short half-hours, I believe, were all that the two were able to have together during the fortnight that remained. One regrets now all the more that time prevented the carrying out of Mr. Nicholson's friendly suggestion. He had known Mallory for some years, ever since the latter had been the best man at his daughter's wedding with Robert Graves, and a 'record' from the hand of Mr. Nicholson, painted at his own wish, might now have been a precious possession.

Mallory sailed in the S.S. *California* from Liverpool on February 28th, and once the farewells were over his letters show that about everything connected with the expedition itself his optimism was continually in the ascendant. In one respect he was especially happy: again and again he speaks of his companions in tones of the strongest appreciation and affection, and it is abundantly clear that he felt the party to be almost an ideal combination. But this was later on, for the full company only assembled at Darjeeling; on the boat he had company, too much of it, but of a different kind. 'This is a fine big ship, steady and comfortable, but overcrowded; we swarm on the deck like ants and sit elbow to elbow reading and writing. . . . The best sight on the way out after Gibraltar, which nothing can beat, will be the white Sierra Nevada and the Atlas Mountains; another good sight will be the backs of three-quarters of our number when they leave the ship at Port Said, bound for Egypt and King Tutankhamen's tomb, or the nearest they can get to it. How, think you, would King Tut have regarded our friends from Glasgow? Nearly every one on the ship, stewards, sailors, cabin-boys, officers, even to the captain himself, come from that centre of civilization beyond the Tweed. How the Scotch contrive to fill the smallest detail with emphasis and character! They surely deserve to succeed, and succeed they do, and how hateful is success! Still, there they sit, very competently and, no doubt, usefully in all the best jobs in the east where trade is concerned, and if they are often too provincial to make their communications very interesting they at least avoid becoming superior persons. But I wish they would talk our language, or at least not the Glasgow variety of theirs. Luckily I get on with it fairly well as I learnt a good many of the sounds in the war, when I was with the Clyde R.G.A.'

'I've just been reading André Maurois's *Ariel*', he writes in a letter to Mr. Benson on the same day. 'It has been much talked of, I understand, and one sees the reason of that, and so far as Shelley's matrimonial and unmatrimonial adventures are exploited for an easy success the book is objectionable; but Maurois has a good deal of intuition, and his description of Harriet Westbrook and condemnation of Godwin are both good I think. And he does bring out Shelley's whole relation to society and the nature of his rebellion. I suppose there is little in the book that is new? It is curious how, reading the episodes of the life detached from the stories of manners, the weight of sadness in it comes out and brings one constantly back to expressions of sadness in the poems. I've luckily got a little volume of Shelley with me and mean to spend some time reading it carefully.'

The journey across India was ' a very grimy, dusty business, and I was glad to get to the end of our train journeying. The hot weather apparently came with a rush this year, just before we landed, and the temperature must have been up to 100° a good part of the time we were in the train.' This was from Darjeeling, during their short stay there from Friday to Wednesday, much taken up with packing and other arrangements. And he says in another letter: 'Norton has got the whole organization under his hand and we shall economize much time and money by dumping some of our boxes en route; all the stores for the high camps have practically been settled already. He is going to be an ideal second to Bruce.

'The party looks very fit altogether. Somervell and Odell, besides the General, Geoffrey Bruce, and Norton, were here before us; it was very nice to see Somervell again and Odell is one of the best. Really it is an amazingly good party altogether. I like especially Hingston, our M.O., an Irishman, a quiet little man and a very keen naturalist. The only one I don't know yet is Shebbeare, who belongs to the Forestry Department and is said to be a particularly nice man. We go to-morrow to Kalimpong altogether, as before, and then separate into two parties; I shall be with the second, with Norton, Hingston, Irvine, and Shebbeare I believe. Noel's movements are independent; he is more than ever full of stunts: the latest is a Citroën tractor which somehow or another is to come into Tibet—a pure *ad.* of course!

'Four of us walked up to Seneschal Hill yesterday afternoon to see the magnolias. They were magnificent—a better show than last year—four different sorts, of white and deep cerise-pink and two lighter pinks between. They do look startlingly bright on a dark hillside.'

Mallory also wrote while in Darjeeling to his sister who was living in Ceylon. 'It has occurred to me that you can be very useful to us! Of all things we shall want to know when to expect the monsoon, and we may be able to get an idea as to whether it is late or early, and by how many days, if you can supply information as to what the monsoon is doing in Ceylon; so I want you to do three things.

'(1) Find out the average date for the beginning of the monsoon in Colombo.

'(2) Write about once in five days a p.c. to say what the weather is doing—e. g. "Heavy cloud, rain expected" or "clear sky after three days' intermittent rain" or whatever it may be. Date of course required.

'(3) Send a wire to me at Chomolung-Phari as soon as it is absolutely certain that the first heavy rain of the monsoon has started in Ceylon.

' Since writing the above I have just been talking to Norton who agrees that this information may be very valuable to us, and he suggests a fourth thing—sometime, perhaps a week or ten days after the monsoon begins it is generally known whether it is *light, heavy,* or *normal strength*; we ought to know that too; it might make a vital difference to our plans—so will you also telegraph that information? The Monsoon must be at least three weeks earlier with you so there should be a considerable margin of time, as we have a specially speedy postal service arranged this time, for us to get warning from your p.c.'s and telegrams.

EVEREST

'All the party is assembled here but one, who is at Kalimpong. It is really a topping good party this year with no duds I think. Norton is in great form as second-in-command arranging things admirably, and we're all very fit by the looks of us. I have to get my English mail off to-day, so no more now.'

The first stages of the march were uneventful. From Rangli Chu he wrote, on March 29th, ' This is the great day of valley-ease and warmth and languor and the delights of the lotus-eater, and I must write to you here with my feet in the splashing stream and heaven all about me as I look up. We started from Pedong this morning—sloped easily down the 2,000 feet to the stream where I bathed last time while Noel immortalized the event; [1] there Irvine, Odell, and I bathed, properly this time, even finding a pool to dive into, and at length. Thence on ponies up to Rheenok—you should be able to follow all this on one of my old maps of Sikkim— where I made some attempt at photographing the remarkable houses, and thence not up over the pass by Ari to get here by the shortest way, but contouring the hill until we could drop into this valley six miles below the bungalow. It is a very lovely valley, quite one of the best parts of Sikkim and we had a good walk up, quite energetically carrying heavy rucksacks. I was wearing my new boots for the

[1] This refers to the cinematograph film which had been shown at his lectures on the second expedition. It was a poor sort of bathe, of a decorum suited more to its destined publicity than to the pools of Sikkim; hence the *properly* in the following sentence.

first time for a whole march and found them pretty comfortable, my ankle and hip and all going quite well too, so that I quite expect by the time we reach Phari I shall have ceased to think about them. The weather is perfectly fine but very hazy, owing to the great number of fires in the valleys. It is the custom of this country to burn a good deal of dead leaves and undergrowth in the forests in order to get better new grass in the spring—but I can't remember anything like so much haze as this last year. Consequently we have had nothing at all of a view all the way from Darjeeling. I hear there has been exceptionally little snow in Tibet and the plains are already beginning to look green—but this is hardly credible.

' It has, apart from views, been a pleasant journey so far. We started in motors for six miles from Darjeeling and half-way down the hill Norton, Hingston, Somervell, and self had breakfast with a tea-planter called Lister—it is a famous tea-garden I believe, and he certainly gave us to drink Orange Pekoe of the most delicious flavour. After that pleasant interval we took all the short cuts hurrying down to Tista Bridge, where we arrived dripping and found our ponies; my pony which is to carry me to Phari is quite a good beast—the best I have had at this stage and my saddle is comfortable and I feel very well off altogether; we went straight up the hill on our ponies and were in Kalimpong at 1.30 for tiffin.

' At Kalimpong next day last time's performances were repeated—a " tamasha " for boy scouts and girl guides and a wonderful little ceremony in the big schoolroom with all of us on the platform singing the metrical version of Psalm 121 to the tune of the Old Hundredth, and prayers, and speech-making divinely mixed. Old Dr. Graham is really a wonder, and if one were going to be a missionary one couldn't do better. He has between 600 and 700 children, mostly bastards or children of ne'er-do-well parents, and does them well all round. When the old Scot is short of money he goes down to Calcutta and collects a few lakhs of rupees from the big business men, who all know and believe in him, and so his institutions flourish.

'I think I told you the names of the second party, but omitted Odell. Shebbeare the forest officer is an excellent fellow; we went a little walk into the forest above Pedong last evening and we saw quite close a very fine jungle cat, about as high as Raven [1] but with the proportions of Agapanthus,[2] which it also resembled in colour—Shebbeare didn't get a very good view of it and couldn't tell me what it was; but it is extraordinary how it makes the whole forest seem alive to see a beast like that. We couldn't be a nicer party—at least I hope the others would say the same; we go along our untroubled way in the happiest fashion.

'Since I began writing the air has become unbearably stuffy and a thunderstorm is brewing. The one crab about this place is that there is no water-supply which is at all likely to be unpolluted—and so one drinks tea, but our tiffin-tea has left me very

[1] A Labrador retriever dog.   [2] A cat.

THE LAST ADVENTURE

thirsty and I long for a long lemon squash or whisky and soda. You see how completely a physical animal one has become.

'I'm spending a certain amount of time and effort as we come along learning Hindustani; it is very unsatisfactory because the coolies themselves are so bad at it; but I do find already that I get on with them more easily. We shall be very short of men who can speak to porters higher up, Irvine, Odell, Beetham, none of them know a word yet.

'I'm really enjoying myself now with a good holiday feeling. To-morrow's march is all uphill to Sedongchen and the next, still up, to Gnatong (12,500), is the great Rhododendron march, but only the very lowest will be in flower.

'I have in mind another little *détour*, by way of variety, from Kupup, diverging to the Natu La instead of Jelap La as before.'

The next news is from Yatung, Tibet, April 2nd. 'Here all goes well—to perfection even. Delightful sunny days in Sikkim, charming companions and these last days a good appetite. Oh! I was glad to see behind me the confinement of the voyage, the hot, dusty journey across India and even the tiresomeness of packing and getting off in Darjeeling. Here we have an interlude, a high Alpine valley with conifers, freshly green interposed between the subtropical forests and the plains of Tibet. In two marches we shall reach Phari, and there will not be a bush nor a green blade of anything to be seen.

'I think I told you before that I had finished *Ariel* with great delight. Since then I have been reading again some of Shelley's poems, and also reading some I had never read before—e. g. *Queen Mab* and the *Cenci*. It is extraordinary how much more of the prophet and how much less of the artist he was at the start. I can read *Queen Mab* because I am interested in Shelley's mind, but it is poor stuff *qua* poetry, and so are the *Masque of Anarchy* and the *Cenci*.

' I have also with me a volume of Keats's Letters (not the Sydney Colvin edition, which leaves out most of the best, but one edited by Buxton Forman and recently reprinted in a cheap edition); there's no better reading, if you can read great men's letters at all. Personally I can hardly conceive the state of mind when one couldn't. I wish there were a thousand volumes of Keats's Letters.

' But I am writing to you as though I were a being on fire with intellectual passion, and the truth is that I have become just an animal, and I am glad to be an animal, with an appetite and strong limbs and a wonderful capacity for sleep and for silence and for simple pleasant dreams. Thus I leave you, to go and lay my head on my little square pillow and so perhaps decrease the infinite distance between this land and England more a thousand times in the twinkling of an eye half-closed towards sleep, than I can by all the summoning of my friends to the front of what the mind's eye sees as I sit writing to them.'

In another letter of the same date, he writes, ''All goes well with me. The march from Sedongchen to Gnatong was glorious, Kanchenjunga and his neighbours appearing magnificently; I haven't seen any distant mountain view before from this part and we counted ourselves very lucky. Gnatong (12,500 feet) was not so cold this time, though the verandah was bunged up with snow, and from there we made two easy stages here, to Yatung, stopping the night in a little rest house an hour down this side of the Jelap La. Norton and I walked up to the pass (14,500 feet) together and were pleased to think that we felt fitter than last year. I certainly am feeling very fit now. I sleep long and well and can walk as fast as any one. We have had a few good signs of spring—on the Sikkim side a most lovely little primula flourishing from 9,000 to 11,000, with the habit of our English primrose, only somewhat smaller and neater—and of a delicious crimson colour; and Rhododendron Falconeri, a big bright red fellow, was flowering freely a bit lower. On this side we have another primula, Denticulata, paler in colour and of the polyanthus type, very freely scattered over the meadows; and we have our old friend Daphne. I know not what species. The conifers too in this valley are all showing green.

'It has been a wonderfully pleasant journey so far, with bright sun and pleasant conditions altogether. And it has been a very jolly company. We found the first contingent here no less happy than ourselves. The General (*entre nous*) has not been quite well and has stayed here to-day while Norton takes on the first party. The slack day here has been very pleasant. I have had a long ramble with Irvine.'

His next letter is dated April 7th, one march beyond Phari Dzong. 'I stupidly didn't write from Phari—not realizing that I should probably have no chance of sending a letter back on the way to Kampa. But it happens there may be a chance to-morrow, so I will write a few lines in bed to-night. It isn't easy to write because the site of my tent dips slightly towards the head of my bed and no amount of propping seems quite to overcome the difficulty. If I had my bed the other way round my head would be at the mouth of the tent and this would create a difficulty about light; besides it is snowing slightly and may snow more, and though I don't mind having my feet snowed upon for the sake of fresh air, I am unwilling to have my head snowed upon during the night. As it is my tent is a wonderfully comfortable spot. The little table made for me by our friend in Maid's Causeway is at my bedside and on it my reading lamp; I expect I shan't always be able to have oil for this, but so long as I can I shall burn it. Did I tell you about the Whymper tents? We each have one to himself. They have two poles like this ∧ at each end, a much more convenient plan than the other with a single pole; a ground-sheet is sewn into the side so that draught and dust are practically excluded if one pitches in the right direction; and, a great blessing, the tent has plenty of pockets; moreover, it is by no means small—7 feet square or very near it. The mess tent also is a great improvement on last year's; there is ample head room and the mess-servants can pass round without hitting one on the head with the dishes; the tables are wooden (three-ply wood varnished) and it is supposed that messes will be wiped off without difficulty; and they fit conveniently round the poles. The lamps, which burn paraffin vapour (assisted by some clockwork arrangement inside) are also good and an enormous improvement on the dim hurricane lamps used last time. In short a certain amount of care and forethought (chiefly Norton's) has made us much more comfortable without spending a great deal of money.

'I must tell you how wonderfully fit I have been these last days, much better at this stage I'm sure than either in '21 or '22. I feel full of energy and strength and walk uphill here already almost as in the Alps; I sleep long and well; my digestion is good, and in short I haven't a trouble physically, unless one may count my ankle of which I'm often conscious, but the leg seems perfectly strong and I'm sure it won't let me down.

'The General is not coming with us to Kampa Dzong (last year's route, but in six days instead of four) but by another way which will allow him to camp lower. It is difficult to know how much to make of this trouble (don't mention it); I think it is ten to one he will be all right.

'I can't write much more in this position and my arms are getting cold. I was going to tell you something about our plans but I will leave that until the next letter.'

During the march of the next few days, to Kampa Dzong, Mallory was for a time unwell and his condition gave some anxiety, as appendicitis was feared. Happily the trouble cleared off quickly and did not return. It was during a two days' rest at Kampa

Dzong that news came that General Bruce would not be rejoining the expedition. In consequence Lt.-Col. Norton took command and appointed Mallory second-in-command in his place, and also leader of the climbers. For some time before this Norton and Mallory had discussed the detailed plans for climbing the mountain, and they had held conflicting views as to the best organization of forces for the attack. At Kampa Dzong Mallory was very busy formulating a plan, and in a letter below he gives details of it in the form in which it was ultimately adopted. Norton has generously written that ' To Mallory goes all the credit of evolving, from the conflicting views held up to date by him and me, a plan which combined all the good points of both.'

After the warm and pleasant days of rest at Kampa Dzong Mallory ' was able to feel definitely this morning that my trouble has passed. The tenderness in my gut is no longer sensitive, like an old bruise rather, and I feel strong and full of energy, and myself, and I haven't the least doubt I shall remain fit: I shall take every care to do so. I'm happy and find myself harbouring thoughts of love and sympathy for my companions. With Norton of course I shall work in complete harmony; he is really one of the best. I read little, what with Hindustani words and Sherpa names to learn, but I have occasional hours with Keats's letters or the *Spirit of Man*, which give perhaps more pleasure here than at home.'

From Tinki Dzong, on April 17th, he wrote of his plans for climbing the mountain. ' This is only

THE LAST ADVENTURE

a hurried line at the end of a full day to tell you that my tummy is in perfect order again, and I feel as fit as possible. It was a funny go altogether and quite inexplicable. Naturally there was a small appendicitis scare as the tenderness was on the right side, but Somervell was practically sure from the start that I was free from that.

'I've had a brain-wave—no other word will describe the process by which I arrived at another plan for climbing the mountain:

'(a) A. & B. with 15 porters (about) starting from Camp IV (North Col) establish Camp V, building emplacements for 4 tents at about 25,500, and descend.

'(b) C. & D., gasless party, go to Camp V with another 15 porters of whom 7 carry loads and descend; the other 8 go up without loads, practically speaking, and sleep.

'(c) C. & D. proceed to establish a camp VII at 27,300 (about) with these 8 porters carrying up 6 loads.

'(d) E. & F., gas party, on the same day as (c) start with 10 porters (about) from Camp IV, go without loads to Camp V, and from that point, E. & F. using oxygen, they take on the stores and gas previously dumped at V about 1,000 feet higher to VI at 26,500.

'(e) The two parties start next morning and presumably meet on the summit.

'You will readily perceive the chief merits of this plan: the mutual support which the two parties can give each other; the establishment of camps without waste of reserve climbers (A. & B. will not have done so much that they can't recover); the much better chance this way of establishing Camp VI without collapse of porters. And then if this go fails we shall be in the best possible position to decide how the next attempt should be made; four climbers we hope will be available and the camps either way will be all ready.

'This plan has such great advantages over all others that Norton has taken it up at once and this evening we had another pow-wow and every one has cordially approved. I'm much pleased about this, as you may imagine—if only for this it seems worth while to have come; for in this plan, I'm sure, there is much greater safety. It is impossible yet to say who the parties will be. Norton and I have talked about it; he thinks Somervell and I should each lead one of these two parties; he puts himself in my hands as to whether he should be one of them—isn't that generous? We shall have to judge as best we can of people's fitness when we reach the Base Camp. Either Odell or Irvine must be of the gas party.'

Two days later, on April 19th, came the first news from Colombo, and indications that the season was likely to be an abnormal one. 'I heard from Mary to-day with news of the weather in Colombo and it looks as if the earliest breath of the monsoon is a fortnight early! But that doesn't necessarily mean much. The bad sign is the weather here which is distinctly more unsettled than in '22, and these last two nights have been unhealthily warm. To-day we

THE LAST ADVENTURE

have been in a regular storm area though no rain or snow has actually fallen here.'

After an interval of five days he continues at Shekar Dzong. 'I've left it rather late to go on with this letter. That is partly because one way or another I have been spending a good many spare moments on the elaboration of our plans. The difficult work of allotting tasks to men has now been done—Norton and I consulted and he made a general announcement after dinner two days ago. The question as to which of the first two parties should be led by Somervell and which by me was decided on two grounds: (1) on the assumption that the oxygen party would be less exhausted and be in the position of helping the other, it seemed best that I should use oxygen and be responsible for the descent; (2) it seemed more likely on his last year's performance that Somervell would recover after a gasless attempt to be useful again later. It was obvious that either Irvine or Odell should come with me in the first gas-party. Odell is in charge of the gas, but Irvine has been the engineer at work on the apparatus—what was provided was full of leaks and faults and he has practically invented a new instrument, using up only a few of the old parts and cutting out much that was useless and likely to cause trouble; moreover the remaining parties had to be considered and it wouldn't do to make Irvine the partner of Geoffrey Bruce as they would lack mountaineering experience; and so Irvine will come with me. He will be an extraordinarily stout companion, very capable with the gas and with cooking apparatus.

EVEREST

' Norton if he is fit enough will go with Somervell or, if he seems clearly a better goer at the moment, Hazard. Beetham is counted out for the moment, though he's getting fitter. Odell and Geoffrey Bruce will have the important task of fixing Camp V at 25,500.

' The whole difficulty of fitting people in so that they take a part in the assault according to their desire or ambition is so great that I can't feel distressed about the part that falls to me. The gasless party has the better adventure, and as it has always been my pet plan to climb the mountain gasless with two camps above the Chang La it is naturally a bit disappointing that I shall be with the other party. Still the conquest of the mountain is the great thing, and the whole plan is mine and my part will be a sufficiently interesting one and will give me perhaps the best chance of all of getting to the top. It is almost unthinkable with this plan that *I* shan't get to the top; I can't see myself coming down defeated. And I have very good hopes that the gasless party will get up; I want all four of us to get there, and I believe it can be done. We shall be starting by moonlight if the morning is calm and should have the mountain climbed, if we're lucky, before the wind is dangerous.

' This evening four of us have been testing the oxygen apparatus, and comparing the new arrangements with the old. Irvine has managed to save weight, 4 or 5 lb., besides making a much more certain as well as more convenient instrument. I was glad, to find I could easily carry it up the hill, even without using the gas, and better of course with it. On steep ground where one has to climb more or less the load is a great handicap and at this elevation a man is better without it. The weight is about 30 lb., rather less. There is nothing in front of one's body to hinder climbing and the general impression I have is that it is a perfectly manageable load. My plan will be to carry as little as possible, go fast and rush the summit. Finch and Bruce tried carrying too many cylinders.

'I'm still very fit and happy. Tibet is giving us many beautiful moments. With these abnormal weather conditions it is much warmer than in '22 and the whole journey is more comfortable. It is nice having one's own pony—mine is a nice beast to ride, but he's not in good condition, and to-day has had a nasty attack of colic; however he'll have a long holiday to come soon and I hope he'll fatten up and arrive fit and well in Darjeeling, where I shall sell him. Only four marches, starting to-morrow morning, to the Rongbuk monastery! We're getting very near now. On May 3rd four of us will leave the Base Camp and begin the upward trek and on May 17th or thereabouts we should reach the summit. I'm eager for the great events to begin.

'Now I must say Good Night to you and turn into my cosy sleeping bag, where I shall have a clean nose sheet to-night, one of the two you made to fix with patent fasteners. Considering how much grease my face requires, and gets, that device has been very useful.

EVEREST

'The telegram announcing our success if we succeed will precede this letter I suppose: but it will mention no names. How you will hope that I was one of the conquerors! And I don't think you'll be disappointed.'

Rongbuk Base Camp, April 30, 1924.

'We've had unexpected notice of a home-bound mail to-morrow and I've no letter ready. We arrived here only yesterday, and I have been busy ever since, the reason for this is in part that we have arranged for our army of Tibetan coolies to carry our loads up the glacier to No. 2 camp; 150 have actually gone up to-day; consequently we have had a great rush getting our loads ready to go up. My special concern has been with the high-climbing stores and provisions for high camps. Yesterday morning as the animals arrived here I got hold of the boxes I wanted, most of which I knew by sight, and from among the feet of the donkeys and yaks had them carried to a place apart. So I was able to get ready 30 loads, apart from food stores, yesterday afternoon. Later Norton and I had a long pow-wow about the whole of our plan as affects the porters. It is a very complicated business to arrange the carrying to the high camps while considering what the porters have been doing and where, during the previous ten days, so as to have sufficient regard to their acclimatization and fitness: further one has to consider the filling up of Camp III which will still be going on after we have begun the carrying to Camp IV; the accommodation at the various camps; and finally the escorting of porters from Camp III upwards. However I have made a plan for the porters which fits in with that previously made for climbers, and though a plan of this kind must necessarily be complicated it allows for a certain margin and even a bad day or two won't upset our applecart. Irvine and I with Beetham and Hazard start from here on May 3, and after resting a day at Camp III the last two will establish Camp IV, while Irvine and I have a canter up to about 23,000 feet up the East ridge of Changtse, partly to get a better look at camping sites on the mountain, and partly to have a trial run and give me some idea of what to expect from Irvine. Beetham and Hazard, two days later, will escort the first lot of loads to Camp IV; Odell and Geoffrey Bruce the second, establishing Camp V on the following day; Norton and Somervell, and lastly Irvine and self follow; Irvine and I will get two or three days down at Camp I meanwhile.

'The Rongbuk Valley greeted us with most unpleasant weather. The day before yesterday and the following night when we were encamped outside the Rongbuk Monastery a bitterly cold wind blew, the sky was cloudy and finally we woke to find a snow storm going on. Yesterday was worse, with light snow falling most of the day. However to-day has been sunny after a windy night, and the conditions on Everest have gradually improved until we were saying to-night that it would have been a pleasant evening for the mountain. It is curious that though quite a considerable amount of snow has fallen during these last few days and the lower slopes are well-covered, the upper parts of Everest appear scarcely affected—that is a phenomenon we observed often enough in 1922, and notably on the day when we made the first attempt.

'We continue to be a very pleasant party. Beetham has had a truly marvellous recovery but I can't quite believe in his being really strong yet, though he makes a parade of energy and cheerfulness, and I'm a little doubtful about his being one of the first starters.

'I'm very fit—perhaps not just so absolutely a strong goer as in '21 but good enough I believe—and anyway I can think of no one in this crowd stronger, and we're a much more even crowd than in '22, a really strong lot Norton and I are agreed. It would be difficult to say of any one of the eight that he is likely to go farther or less far than the rest. I'm glad the first blow lies with me. We're not going to be easily stopped with an organization behind us this time.'

The next letter is to his sister in Ceylon, who had sent reports of the monsoon, as arranged.

Rongbuk Base Camp, May 3, 1924.

'It seems ages ago since I received your letter and two postcards. All that you told me about the monsoon was of great interest. This seems the most extraordinary season compared with previous experience of Tibet. The atmosphere has been just as it is during the monsoon and much warmer than in '22; we have to prepare for an early monsoon, though I daresay these conditions may only tend to delay it. At present the mountain is very windy and sprinkled with fresh snow and looks most unpleasant for climbing; it has been quite cold besides up here these last days. I look forward to your next news, but the mail seems to be delayed for ever. I can't tell you how full of hope I am this year. It is all so different from '22, when one was always subconsciously dissatisfied because we had no proper plan of climbing the mountain. And this year it has been a chief object with Norton and me to organize the whole show as it should be organized—[*Here the letter continues in pencil*]—Sorry the ink has begun to freeze! And now we've really got a plan (my plan incidentally) which seems to give good chances of success. . . . And here I am at Camp II (I could not get on with this letter at the Base Camp) in the first stages of carrying it out. The final assault on or about May 17 will be with two parties of two, one with and one without oxygen—the respective two being Irvine and myself and Somervell and Norton. The difficult personal questions have all been arranged in the friendliest possible manner. The plan of course had to come first, and a most important part of it is leaving an adequate reserve—equal in strength to the vanguard—to make other assaults if the first parties fail. Now the first great difficulty is in establishing the highest camps, and for that previous experience is of great importance. It was easily decided, therefore, that Somervell and I should each lead one of the first two parties. Naturally each wanted to go without oxygen; but on last time's performance it looks as though Somervell after going without gas will be more likely than me to recover for a second attempt; and Norton considers me a good companion for Irvine who has had little mountaineering experience. He'll be a splendid companion; he is a mechanical genius and a tower of strength and an absolutely sound fellow right through, and he'll go well on the mountain and make no rash or silly steps. I somehow feel as if we were going to get there this time. And I believe Somervell and Norton, who will have two camps above 23,000 against our one, have a very fair chance of getting there too. Norton, besides being a hard man to beat, will be immensely useful in getting the porters up to 27,000—he speaks their lingo as none of the rest of us do except Geoffrey Bruce. Well then, on May 17th the four of us should join up somewhere about the base of the final pyramid—and whether we get up or not it will be my job to get the party off the mountain in safety—and I'm keen about that part too—no one climber or porter is going to get killed if I can help it—that would spoil all.

'It is May 4th and I'm in bed, the only tolerable place about 8 p.m. I shan't sleep again under 21,000 until we've had our whack—plenty of time for acclimatization, and meanwhile I shall be seeing through our elaborate bandobast, counting loads up to the North Col, &c. I can barely see by this single candle lantern, so Good night—I've good hope of seeing you if we can get the mountain climbed early.'

Here the letter should have ended; but it was

continued after an interval of nearly two weeks, on May 16th, the day before he had seen the four of them, in his hopeful vision, at the base of the final pyramid. Of what had happened in the interval I will give the shortest possible account.

The day after Mallory lay writing by the light of his candle lantern, he had started with Odell, Hazard, and Irvine and twenty porters to establish Camp III at 21,000 feet beneath the icy slopes of the North Col. Three days later at 6 p.m. the last of this pioneer party came staggering through the seracs of the glacier, back to Camp II, a routed company. So terrible had been the cold and the icy winds they had experienced that, in Norton's words, Mallory ' had practically to man-handle many men out of the tents on to their feet, so completely had the hardships taken the heart out of them.'

This was on May 7th. On May 9th Mallory started again for Camp III, this time with Norton and Geoffrey Bruce. There was still a gale blowing, and this soon brought with it a blizzard which lasted forty-eight hours. On the morning of the 10th the party awoke to find their tents filled with inches of powdery snow. On the 11th, after another night of cold and hurricane, Col. Norton gave orders for a general retreat to the Base Camp for recuperation, and this was completed by 2 p.m. on the 12th.

On May 16th the letter to his sister was continued:

'There's been never a chance all this while of dispatching this letter and meanwhile I've had a letter and a postcard from you, and before you get this you will have read news of our reverse. The weather was really impossible—and as we must have our porters fit and happy to do any good when it comes to the point of attack, the only possible plan was to retreat and wait. Now the weather looks better—but the first possible day for reaching the summit is May 28th instead of May 17th, and if the monsoon is early we may get caught. We shall be going up the glacier again to-morrow—the old gang once more the vanguard. I'm afraid the chances of seeing you are disappearing down the Tibetan wind at this rate.'

The following is of the same date, May 16th:

' My last letters—and one came from you—were dated round about March 25th. You may imagine how one feels cut off. And long before you get this you will have read the story of our reverses when first we went up the glacier, and perhaps the stories of our next advance which will begin to-morrow.... We had a pretty hard time at Camp III those days, the conditions much more severe than in '22. It is pitiful to see men done to the world and helpless, and its hard work, too, driving them to look after themselves. One of them will be very lucky if he doesn't lose both feet, and yet, if he had looked after himself, he would not have been frost-bitten at all. I've been lucky myself, fit and energetic at the crucial times—I shouldn't like to feel that any one was conspicuously stronger than me—I don't!

' You've no idea how complicated and difficult all the organization is this time. I find myself doing

THE LAST ADVENTURE

a lot of hard mental work thinking out the details of our plan: which loads are to be carried where and when, and what porters must be available; and without much detailed planning we should land ourselves in hopelessness and be asking too much of the porters. We believe it is just possible for them to do what we want them to do, and everything has to be arranged to give them the best chance of doing it. The crucial matter is the fixing of the highest camps; provided that can be done, I believe we'll get to the top.

'It is a bit disappointing to me that my part turns out to be with the oxygen. I had always hoped to get up without it. However, the management of all that happens above Camp III is in my hands, so I have a good part altogether.'

Although the weather had cut short this first advance before any of the detailed plans for climbing the upper slopes of the mountain could be put into action, yet their severe experiences had at least served as a test of the porters' quality, and had brought to the fore certain of the strongest and most reliable men. All camps below the North Col were now established, moreover, and partially stocked. Ever since the reassembly at the Base Camp on May 12th Mallory had been busy recasting plans for the second advance, setting out in minutest detail the movements of each climber and each party of porters during the next ten days. The original plan from the North Col upwards was to be adhered to, and although the party had suffered severely, and the final attempt on the summit would be deferred from the 17th until about the 29th of May, yet there was at this stage no reason to feel that the chances of reaching the top had sensibly diminished.

The delay was serious, for weather reports had hinted, as we have seen, at the possibility of an early monsoon. In 1922 it had broken on June 1st. This year, as it turned out, it did not arrive in earnest until about June 15th, but the season was unique in the experience of the oldest planters in Darjeeling, and the Himalayas were repeatedly swept by storms during the second half of May, which, although actually not connected with the monsoon current, seemed to presage its immediate arrival. All plans after the first advance from the Base Camp were affected by this sense of a race with the monsoon. It was this which forced upon the expedition the necessity of establishing themselves upon the North Col without waiting for suitable weather, in order to seize the first fine interval for launching the attack upon the summit.

The morning of May 16th was brilliantly fine, with the mountain clear and serene, and a start next day was decided upon. Not yet, however, was the mountain deserted by its ally the weather. Ten days later the whole party were again at the Base Camp after a second reverse. A way had this time been forced to the North Col and a camp established, but only to be evacuated the next day as a result of snow-storms, wind, and a temperature which fell to minus 24° F. 'It has been a bad time altogether', Mallory wrote on May 27th. 'I look back on tremendous effort and exhaustion and dismal looking out of a

THE LAST ADVENTURE

tent door into a world of snow and vanishing hopes. And yet there have been a good many things to set on the other side. The party has played up wonderfully.'

The establishment of a route to the North Col on May 20th had been the work of Norton, Mallory, and Odell. The line taken and the difficulties of the route differed widely from those of two years before: the comparatively easy route of 1922 on which the fatal avalanche occurred had to be avoided, and this involved the crossing of a fault in the lip of a huge crevasse which formed a defence work right across the steep slopes to the north of the old route. The technical difficulties of cutting steps in, and climbing, the nearly vertical ice walls of the fault were more serious than anything else encountered at these altitudes—they would have been serious in the Alps—but, to quote Col. Norton's account—' confronted with a serious climbing obstacle Mallory's behaviour was always characteristic: you could positively see his nerves tighten up like fiddle strings. Metaphorically he girt up his loins, and his first instinct was to jump into the lead. Up the wall and chimney he led here, climbing carefully, neatly, and in that beautiful style that was all his own. I backed him up close below, able now and then to afford him a foothold with haft or head of my axe.' For the last 200 feet of the climb to the shelf of Camp IV, the way led diagonally up a snow slope at the extreme angle on which snow would lie. Up this slope, in spite of his earlier exertions, Mallory again took the lead, cutting steps in the half-ice, half-snow surface. The shelf was successfully reached at 2.30 p.m., and now 'nothing' would please the indomitable Mallory but that the route onwards from our shelf to the actual col must be reconnoitred, and Odell at once volunteered to lead the way '. The task proved the affair of a long hour, and Mallory was nearly at the end of his tether when he and Odell returned.

Of this climb and of the descent after it Mallory gives some account in the last long letter which he wrote, seven days later, from the Base Camp. ' The first visit to the North Col was a triumph for the old gang. Norton and I did the job, and the cutting of course was all my part; so far as one can enjoy climbing above Camp III, I enjoyed the conquest of the ice wall and crack, the crux of the route, and the making steps too in the final steep 200 feet. Odell did very useful work leading the way on from the camp to the Col; I was practically bust to the world and couldn't have led that half-hour although I still had enough mind to direct him. We made a very bad business of the descent. It suddenly occurred to me that we ought to see what the old way down was like. Norton and I were ahead unroped, and Odell in charge of a porter who had carried up a light load. We got on to ground where a practised man can just get along without crampons (which we hadn't with us) chipping occasional steps in very hard snow or ice. I was all right ahead, but first Norton had a nasty slip and then the porter, whose knot didn't hold so that he went down some way and was badly shaken. Meanwhile I, below, finding the best way down, had walked into an obvious crevasse; by some miscalculation I had thought I had prodded the snow with which it was choked and where I hoped we could walk instead of cutting steps at the side of it—all the result of mere exhaustion no doubt—but the snow gave way and in I went with the snow tumbling all round me, down luckily only about 10 feet before I fetched up half-blind and breathless to find myself most precariously supported only by my ice-axe somehow caught across the crevasse and still held in my right hand—and below was a very unpleasant black hole. I had some nasty moments before I got comfortably wedged and began to yell for help up through the round hole I had come through, where the blue sky showed—this because I was afraid my operations to extricate myself would bring down a lot more snow and perhaps precipitate me into the bargain. However, I soon grew tired of shouting—they hadn't seen me from above—and bringing the snow down a little at a time I made a hole out towards the side (the crevasse ran down a slope) after some climbing, and extricated myself—but was then on the wrong side of the crevasse, so that eventually I had to cut across a nasty slope of very hard ice, and further down some mixed unpleasant snow, before I was out of the wood. The others were down by a better line ten minutes before me. That cutting against time at the end, after such a day, just about brought me to my limit.'

The weather next day was threatening when the first large party of three climbers, with a convoy of twelve porters laden with tents, stores, and provisions, made their way up the ice staircase to Camp IV.

EVEREST

Fresh fallen snow had all but obliterated the tracks of the pioneers and made the climbing both dangerous and very laborious. The ice chimney was deemed impracticable for a laden porter, and as an alternative Somervell and Irvine hauled the twelve loads, weighing 20 to 30 lb. each, hand over hand up the ice cliff while the porters climbed the chimney unencumbered. Light intermittent showers gave place in the afternoon to a continuous fall of soft wet snow, so that nothing of the North Col slopes could be seen from below. Late in the evening Somervell and Irvine returned to Camp III with the news that the party had reached the Col with their loads, and that Hazard, with the twelve porters, had remained there for the night. Snow continued to fall uninterruptedly until 3 p.m. the next day, May 22nd. There could be no question of a second party starting for the Col, nor of Hazard and his twelve returning. The morning of the 23rd provided a brilliant and short-lived gleam, but it enabled those at Camp III to detect the rows of little black dots moving downwards which told them that Hazard was evacuating the Col. At 5 p.m. he arrived, but with only eight of his twelve men. Four had lost their nerve on the steep traverse just below the camp and had refused to come on. The situation had now become suddenly very serious. Snow was falling steadily, and four men, of whom two were reported frostbitten, were about to spend their third consecutive night on the North Col without any sahib to stimulate them to eat or to look after themselves. Clearly they must be rescued without any delay. This fact alone re-

THE LAST ADVENTURE

duced any chance of success during this second advance practically to vanishing point, and might well mean the abandonment of all further attempt for the year. The whole party at Camp III was far through with cold and lack of sleep, and the business of rescuing four possibly helpless men under such conditions would be a severe tax upon the strongest. That physique which was to have conquered the mountain must needs expend itself on the saving of human lives. At 7.30 a.m. on May 24th, Norton, Mallory, and Somervell, set out. At 7.30 p.m. they returned with the four marooned porters safely to Camp III. What those twelve hours must have meant to men in their exhausted condition, labouring through soft snow liable always to avalanche, and with all the added anxieties of a rescue party, must be left to the imagination of the reader. Even before they started the condition of the rest of the porters had precluded any possibility of pressing the attempt further without a spell for recuperation; and while the rescue was in progress the evacuation of all the high camps had begun for the second time. The rest of Mallory's letter from the Base Camp may here be given. 'My one personal trouble has been a cough. It started a day or two before leaving the Base Camp, but I thought nothing of it. In the high camps it has been the devil. Even after the day's exercise I have described, I couldn't sleep, but was distressed with bursts of coughing fit to tear one's guts—and a headache and misery altogether; besides which of course it has a very bad effect on one's going on the mountain. Somervell also has a cough which started a little later than mine, and he has not been at his physical best. The following day when the first loads were got up to Camp IV in a snow storm Somervell and Irvine must have made a very fine effort hauling loads up the chimney. .... Poor Norton was very hard hit altogether, hating the thought of such a bad muddle (the isolation of the four porters on the North Col), and himself not really fit to start out next day; nor were any of us for that matter, and it looked ten to one against our getting up with all that snow about, let alone getting a party down. I led from the camp to a point some little distance above the flat glacier; the snow wasn't so very bad as there had been no time for it to get sticky; still, that part with some small delays took us three hours; then Somervell took us to where Geoffrey and Odell had dumped their loads the day before, and shortly afterwards Norton took the lead; luckily we found the snow better as we proceeded. Norton alone had crampons and was able to take us up to the big crevasse without step cutting. Here we had half an hour's halt, and about 1.30 I went on again for the steep 200 feet to the point where the big crevasse joins the corridor. From here there were two doubtful stretches. Norton led up the first, while the two of us made good at the corner of the crevasse; he found the snow quite good. Then Somervell led across the final slope (following Hazard's just discernible tracks). Norton and I had an anxious time belaying and it began to be cold, too, as the sun had left us. Somervell made a very good show getting the men off—but I won't

THE LAST ADVENTURE

repeat my report. Time was pretty short as it was 4.30 when they began to come back, using Somervell's rope as a hand rail. Naturally the chimney took some time. It was just dark when we got back to camp.

'Norton has been quite right to bring us down for rest. It is no use sending men up the mountain unfit. The physique of the whole party has gone down sadly. The only chance now is to get fit and go for a simpler quicker plan. The only plumb-fit man is Geoffrey Bruce. Norton has made me responsible for choosing the parties of attack, himself first choosing me into the first party if I like. But I'm quite doubtful if I shall be fit enough, and again I wonder if the monsoon will give us a chance. I don't want to get caught, but our three-day scheme from the Chang La will give the monsoon a good chance. We shall be going up again the day after to-morrow. Six days to the top from this camp!'

The second retreat to the lower camps was virtually the turning point of the expedition. After that it was clearly impossible to work to the plan and time-table upon which so much care and thought had been expended, for that required a certain minimum of climbers and porters which was no longer available. Of their original strength of 55 porters there were by this time no more than 12 to 15 who could be counted upon to reach even the North Col. The rest, although not physically disabled, had quite lost their morale through the unprecedented weather and hardships. The original plan occupied 15 porters to carry tents and stores *up* from Camp IV, so that clearly some much simplified plan must be adopted.

EVEREST

A council of the whole party was held at Camp I on May 27th, and as a result of this ' we decided to scrap oxygen altogether and to assault the mountain in a series of attempts, each of two climbers: the parties to leave Camp IV on consecutive fine days and to sleep twice above that point, once at Camp V at about 25,500 feet, and once at Camp VI at about 27,200 feet, or as near to those heights as we could induce porters to carry for us. I insisted on a supporting party of two climbers to be at Camp IV always, and this seemed to indicate that not more than two attempts could be made, for we could hardly believe that, after what we had already undergone, any one could be found to do more than one really high climb. But here we judged by the standard of 1922, and Mallory and Odell were yet to show us what was to be the standard of 1924.

'In allocating the climbers to these various roles I stipulated that Mallory had the right to join the first party if he wished. His throat was markedly better, and though he had so far borne the brunt of the hardest work, yet the energy and fire of the man were reflected in his every gesture, and none doubted his fitness to go as high as any '.[1]

A short note to me from Camp I was written on May 28th, the day after these plans had been settled. It is, so far as I know, the last thing Mallory wrote for the post, and it reflects only too clearly his anxiety for the outcome of the next few days. 'I can write but one line. We are on the point of moving up again and the adventure appears more

[1] Lt.-Col. Norton in *The Fight for Everest*, 1924, p. 94.

desperate than ever. Many thanks for two letters, the second from Pen y Pass. You'll have news of me from Ruth, I hope. It is good to think of you near at hand in Cambridge. We've had a bad time up to date, and the party is a good deal knocked out altogether. My one trouble personally has been a severe Tibetan cough, very bad for going, and very difficult to get rid of. All sound plans are now abandoned for two consecutive dashes without gas. Geoffrey Bruce and I the first party (provided I'm fit) and Norton and Somervell in the second—old gangers first, but in fact nothing but a consideration of what is likely to succeed has come in. If the monsoon lets us start from Camp IV it will almost certainly catch us on one of the *three* days from there. Bright prospects!'

Of Mallory's first attempt with Bruce on June 2nd, and of Norton and Somervell's magnificent climb to 28,126 feet on June 4th, an account has been given elsewhere and this is not the place to repeat that story in detail. The weather remained clear, but so icy was the wind encountered by the first party that after a night at 25,500 feet, at Camp V, the three porters had shot their bolt and no mortal persuasion could stir them to a further effort. To attempt the mountain from Camp V was unthinkable, and in the circumstances to fall back upon their supports at Camp IV was the only thing to do. That he should have been baulked in the attempt and yet never have been brought near the limits of his own energy! At that stage, and to Mallory, this must have been a maddening disappointment. If the monsoon allowed them one other chance that year it would infallibly be the last, and in thinking how best to make use of the energy that was still in him it was this reflection, one supposes, that led him to decide upon the use of oxygen for the last fatal attempt, with Irvine, on June 8th.

We may speculate, but to no purpose, upon the manner of their death. The data are scanty enough. They slept at Camp VI, 26,800 feet, on the night of June 7th, and were last seen at 12.50 p.m. the next day, going well, but very late on their schedule time, the summit clear before them and 800 feet above. If what has been written of Mallory as a climber has any meaning, then there should be no need to repeat that the responsibility of the leader on a mountain was a part of his religion. ' He had most definitely made up his mind', says Norton, ' that as leader of a party the responsibility lay heavy on him to turn back, however near the summit, in good time to ensure a return to safety.' And yet—and yet—this was the fifth time he had started out to conquer the mountain and would probably be his last. The climbing of it had become an obsession to him. For weeks and months his whole mind had been concentrated on the evolution of plans in their remotest detail, and his body in carrying them out. As we visualize those two on the ultimate slopes soon after the noon of this further day, snatched, as it were, from the very shadow of the expected monsoon; as we see the sun-bathed summit beckoning to them 800 feet above (and that looks little enough); can we see them turning back? ' It was almost impossible to make out ', says Norton again, ' whether he was a tired man or not, for he responded instantly to every call that was made on him.' Did he perhaps in that supreme struggle not know himself that he was a tired man? Did that dominating nervous energy, so characteristic a part of him, drive them upward and onward relentlessly over those shining slopes, to desert them suddenly at the last? It is notorious that the nervous system plays up until it drops. The collapse is complete and absolute. And if they reached the summit? In that moment of achievement may not the strained cord have snapped, and unconsciousness, the natural refuge of the overwrought body, supervened? This for one, would mean the end for both.

When we are tempted to cry out upon the loss of two such lives, it is well for us to try to see Everest as Mallory saw it. To him the attempt was not just an adventure, still less was it an opportunity for record-breaking. The climbing of the mountain was an inspiration because it signified the transcendence of mind over matter. Nowhere as among the high snow and ice is the utter insignificance of man's bodily presence so overwhelming, nowhere as among those mighty masses do his desires and aspirations seem, by comparison, so triumphant. Those two black specks, scarcely visible among the vast eccentricities of nature, but moving up slowly, intelligently, into regions of unknown striving, remain for us a symbol of the invincibility of the human spirit.